NEVER LET GO OF MY HAND

*Dedicated to the memory of my Mammy and Daddy,
Eddie and Mary McCallion; they showed us a love
beyond all human understanding.*

*'If I ever tell you about my past,
it's never because I want you to
feel sorry for me; it's so you can
understand why I am who I am.'*

Unknown

Edited by Mary-Anne McNulty
Design and layout by PJ Design

Back page image: Stephen Latimer Photography

CONTENTS

PART ONE: THE MAKING OF ME

PART TWO: THE LONG DARK TUNNEL

PART THREE: LETTING IN THE LIGHT

PART ONE

THE MAKING
OF ME

Down Memory Lane

My story kicks off on the day I was born: December 15th, 1942. *Or does it?*

My name is Johnny McCallion. I am the first child of Mary McCallion (née McCourt) and Eddie McCallion. Some of my earliest memories (all my early memories, I should say) are of a childhood wrapped up in the love and security provided by my parents. One of the most vivid is of my Daddy carrying me in his arms, wrapped up in a blanket and feeling as snug as a bug in a rug, as we made our way home to Pennyburn, on a dark winter night. I remember so clearly that feeling of warmth and love on that journey from the Lecky Road, then down along the Strand Road, with Mammy (that's her and me on the book's front cover) by our side.

I was left in my Granny's house in 97, Lecky Road during the day while my Mammy went to work in Ritchie's shirt factory and my Daddy to his job in Downey's shoemaker's shop on the Strand Road. I found so much love in this home. There was my 'Da' and 'Ma' (as we called my grandparents), my uncles, Johnny and Alec, my aunt Rose and a very special lady - my aunt Kath. I would go out the town every morning with my Ma; some afternoons, my Da would take me to get me lemonade (and himself a Guinness or stout) in one of the many pubs in the area. This was not a 'pub crawl', you understand; it was just all part of an idyllic life at this time.

I remember sitting at their front door every morning and watching what seemed to be a non-stop procession of horses drawing carts of coal along the Lecky Road on their way to the Gasyard. I also have vivid memories of the many funerals that passed by our door back then; the black hearses, with their magnificent horses, that led the many funerals, and the man with his black caster hat sitting up top.

I remember the neighbours of that time; many of whom were to remain lifelong friends. Sadly, many of the old faces are gone now. Mr and Mrs McQuaide, him with his plug tobacco and pipe. Mr and Mrs Laverty and Mr and Mrs Stewart. James and Ellen McFeely, they ran the local paper shop in their front room. The Houstons, the McIntyres, the McCaffertys, Mrs Donnelly and the Brothers family, Mr and Mrs McBrearty, the Dohertys, the Concannons, Joe Canney, the Ferrys and my childhood friend from those days, Tommy Cullen. Oh, and Mammy's good friend, Kathleen Gallagher, who lived in the locality. All, in their own way, added their bit to making me the man I am today.

Memories flood back of Da toasting my bread on a fork at the range fire (toast doesn't taste like that now), of the smell of Mickey Quigley's fruit and fish shop in William Street and the man who served us there; Stephen Quigley.

At that time I had no idea how much he would later figure in the making of me. I recall our own home at St Patrick's Terrace, in the Pennyburn area of Derry, and of Mammy's friend Frances McCourt (no relation), who had married a man from Walsall, and their son John, who came to visit us. There is a photo somewhere of John and me sitting at the front step. My father's sister, Lizzie, and her husband Tommy also stayed with us until they got a house of their own.

My aunt Rose and the fella who was to become her husband and lifetime companion, Peter Farrenden, figure strongly in my memories of that time. Peter had arrived in Derry as part of the naval fleet coming and going from the docks. I remember her excitement as she prepared for his visits, and going with her down to the Northern Counties Hotel in the town centre so she could meet him. I remember him waving from a window that, to my young mind, seemed to be so high up. I didn't know how he'd gotten there. Rose used to call me her 'Johnny Joe'. She always had a special place in my heart. Peter protected her (up until he could do no better) from the knowledge that he was terminally ill. She died within six or seven months of his death; no will to go on. I am sure, by now, you are sensing the love and care that was (and still is) so central to my being.

In October 1947, a new housing development was beginning to take shape in Derry. It was called the Creggan Estate, and Ma and Da were one of the first to be allocated a home there; at 24 Inishowen Gardens. It must have been like heaven to them because it had a large living room, a scullery, an inside toilet, a bathroom and - lord of lords - three bedrooms plus a front and back garden. So, to Creggan they did go, along with me, Mammy and Daddy, Aunt Rose and Uncle Johnny. I don't know how it was done, but space didn't seem to be a problem and, somehow, there was room for everyone. We weren't officially on the rent book back then, so I often wonder if we could have been classified as the first squatters in Creggan.

When my aunt Rose got married, my only worry was who would now make my birthday cakes. Within a year of Rose's going to England, Mammy told me I was going to get a baby sister. By this time, I had started school and the only other child who had intruded into my territory, up until then, was my cousin Donna. She was my aunt Kath's daughter and we were very close to one other. And then Nuala arrived.

She was two and a half years old and it was great to have her with us. Just like me, she had come from the Nazareth House (I have vague memories of going to the one in Fahan with Mammy to get her). As a young boy of six, the concept of adoption, and the fact that Mammy and Daddy weren't my biological parents, never entered my mind. As far as I was concerned, the Nazareth House was where all babies came from and I never questioned it.

A few weeks after Nuala came, Mammy said we were going to get a brother (some production line, this). I remember her saying the nuns told her not to blame herself if anything happened to him because he was very thin and weak and she could only do her best. Kevin was his name.

Within six weeks, we had become a family of five. Mammy put Kevin in a shoebox beside the open fire to help keep him warm and Da made a cradle with rockers on it so that Daddy could rock him to sleep in the evenings and during the night. It was at this time I heard Daddy sing the one and only song he ever sang: Percy French's 'Come Back Paddy Reilly to Ballyjamesduff'. Ma just spoiled him rotten - everyone had a role in the family.

Life was drifting along and I made my First Holy Communion when I was six and a half years old. The summers seemed to be endless in those days. In my first year at the Rosemount Boys' School, in Helen Street, I was taught by a lady called Miss McVeigh; she was later to marry and become Mrs Carrigan.

My memory of her was how caring she was. I had missed the Christmas party because of illness but she kept my sweets and gave them to Mammy to give to me. In many ways, she laid the foundation stone for my education. I don't think I was ever going to set the world alight academically, but in my world that didn't matter. I met her many times, over the years, after leaving the school, and she never failed to wave to me or ask how everyone was doing.

Another teacher who made a big impression on me was Mary Ann Coyle. Again, it was the way she cared for us - especially those children who may have come from poorer backgrounds. Without any fuss, she made sure that they were near the coal fire and got their fair share of anything that was going. I suspect there was a lot she did that no one else would have been aware of because that was her nature. I hope she (and all caring teachers like her) are never forgotten. I would like to think that, as they sat alone with their memories for days and people long gone, they felt proud of the good work they did.

I was also blessed to have been taught by the late Freddie Campbell and Jim Quinn; both of them were to leave Rosemount and go to the new school, St Patrick's in Pennyburn. Rosemount's loss was certainly St Patrick's gain.

Da, a carpenter by trade, had started work on the homes being built around us. One of my many memories of those summer days (that for some reason never seem to include rain) was of taking his tea up to wherever he was in the site, in the jerry can that Mammy or Ma had prepared for him along with his lunch. I loved going through the buildings; it gave us such a sense of adventure as we played Cowboys and Indians or whatever dramas we thought up at the time. I still look at those homes and think of him.

He loved gardening and planted spuds and all sorts of vegetables in our back garden. Then he started keeping chickens, and I remember it was Christmas time and two of the birds had to be killed for the dinner. No better man than my Da. I don't know if he knew what he was doing, but he cut their heads off and the headless chickens ran around the living room.

Luckily, there were no fitted carpets in those days, as they ran until they dropped dead because no one could or would catch them. Every summer, I only had to go to Inishowen Gardens to be reminded of him because many of the gardens there had a pale pink creeper rose which he had either planted himself or given to some neighbour to plant.

So his memory lives on, because we now have this rose in our garden, taken from the original by Daddy and planted in ours. I hope I am remembered, just like them, for my actions.

It was during those years that Daddy opened his own shoemaker's shop on the Lecky Road, between the Bogside and Wellington Street. Beside it were Hunter's bakery, Semple's milk dairy, the Cabin fish shop and Dinny Harley's hardware shop. I would head down there after school to help him, going to McKeown's in William Street to get the leather and rubber heels and whatever else he needed to carry out his work and run the shop.

My memories of that shop are many and varied. When I look back, my first impression is that it was a meeting place during the day for many unemployed young men of the area, who would come in and sit around the fire and chat away. In those days, unemployment was the main scourge of the town.

The wee shop was also the 'boy meets girl' drop-in centre during the week and the local card school on a Sunday afternoon (no large bets; nobody had any money). Years later, someone who worked for Derry City Council said to me, 'Your father opened the first community centre in Derry, but he never got the wages that people are on today'.

During my time at Rosemount School I struck up a friendship with John Flood. It became one of the most important friendships I have ever had. Life may have taken us in different directions over the years but the seeds of our friendship were firmly rooted during those childhood days.

Sadly, John passed away, suddenly, in 2021. He will always hold a special place in my heart, along with his late mother Fran; if only our hearts were half as big as hers, maybe our country wouldn't be in the mess it's in today.

It was around this time, when I was about nine or ten, that I started to sense something was worrying Mammy. It concerned me, but I didn't know the what or the why.

Sundays were special. We would go to Mass in St Eugene's Cathedral, then, after dinner, my Daddy would take us for a walk. We would usually go to nearby Brooke Park, but occasionally we would head out to Willie White's, a shop just on the other side of the border in Killea in Co Donegal.

This was the late forties and early fifties, the time of butter and sugar shortages after the war, so he was able to smuggle them back. Everyone we knew used to go there, especially during the summer. There is something so relaxing about walking and getting away from the hustle and bustle of everyday living. At that time, the naval ships used to come into Derry quay a lot, and if an especially big one was to arrive, we would all head down to see it. Sometimes we even got on board and got a guided tour.

These are simple memories of a very special man; my Daddy. He did this to give Mammy a rest on a Sunday as she watched us six days a week while he worked to keep us in the style they wanted for us. As far as they were concerned, nothing was ever too much for us.

Who Do People Say I Am?

One day, my cousin Donna and I were playing in the small front bedroom. As we lifted books from the press, a piece of paper fell out from between the pages of one of them. Call it curiosity, nosiness or whatever, but we read it, and suddenly things started to fall into place. It had the following information:

Date of Birth:	15th December 1942
Name:	John Joseph Kelly
Name of Mother:	Rose Kelly
Name of Father:	(Blank)

I looked at the date. *This could be my own birth certificate,* I thought (in hindsight, I think it might actually have been my baptismal lines rather than my birth certificate). It was just the rest of the information on it that didn't make sense. But it did make sense, in a way. The conversations between Mammy and my aunt Kath now took on a new meaning. It was me she was fretting about; about how I would react to what she had to tell me. Even then, I knew how much I loved her and Daddy; nothing or no one else mattered. And sure hadn't I known from a young age that I'd come from the Nazareth House? Though I was now starting to fully understand what that meant, it was still no big deal as far as I was concerned.

But I could see it was playing on Mammy's mind, so I decided to ease her worry. It was a Saturday morning and I was sitting on the workbench beside the cooker as she prepared breakfast (Daddy made it every other day, but he went to the shop early on a Saturday). As she removed the grill pan with the toast on it, I made the big proclamation:

'Mammy, I know.'

She glanced at me. 'What do you know?' she said.

'I know I'm adopted,' I replied. The grill pan hit the ground along with the toast (I often think back to that moment and wonder what I did to her by saying that to her. But, in my mind, I wanted to put an end to her worry). As she recovered, I told her it didn't matter; as far as I was concerned, she was my Mammy. I loved her and Daddy, and no one else mattered.

That day, she told me how special I was to them both. She told me the story of how they had gone to the Nazareth House in Bishop Street to pick a little girl and give her a home filled with love... but fate was to take a hand. A Sr Theresa was walking along the corridor with a little boy; he was due to move on the following day, she told them. But Mammy and Daddy fell in love with me instantly and their search for a wee girl went no further. Mammy would relate this fairy story many times throughout the coming years. Was it a fairy story? Only time would tell. After we had this talk, everything returned to normal and we got on with everyday living.

Around this time, we had another addition to the family: my sister, Marian. She came to us from the Nazareth House in Bishop Street. I can recall her crying, holding on to an old beaten-up teddy bear, afraid to let go of it. Eventually, she settled down and became part of our family of, now, six. Mammy and Daddy never failed to amaze me; here they were adding to the family when they could have chosen to have a carefree lifestyle without the responsibilities of rearing one child, never mind four. They had to go through the process of home visits and I would always detect an uneasiness about Mammy when one of those was due.

She worried a lot and I often heard her say that she wished the adoption was completed and Marian theirs so that there would be no more fear. I wonder did those visitors (and, indeed, their equivalents today) know the fear that a knock at the door from them brought to those inside.

There was one day, I remember, when a visitor was coming from a government agency to interview Mammy and Daddy. Daddy was out at work, incidentally, but she didn't want to talk to these people whether he'd been there or not. So, as the time approached, Mammy made us all keep quiet and when the knock at the door finally resounded throughout the house, you could feel the tension building. By this time, we were all crouched in a corner of the room that the caller couldn't see from the street, even if they were on tiptoe. Silence abounded as we all waited, fearful, with Mammy. Because of that experience, I have a soft spot in my heart for all adoptive parents - especially in this era of change as regards the rights of the birth parents and the increased accessibility of information. A lot of thought should be given to those who adopt.

Around that time, our holidays consisted of Daddy taking the first Monday and Tuesday in August off his work and a picnic being made up. In the earlier years, we would head down the Strand Road to get the train to Buncrana or, in later years when the train had stopped running, to Patrick Street to queue up (along with what seemed to be thousands of people) to get the bus there instead. Back then, a day at the beach was a big occasion.

Then, when I was around thirteen, we took a house for the August fortnight (the customary holiday period in Derry) down in Ballyliffin, in nearby Donegal. There was great excitement in the air as we eagerly prepared for this holiday. Like many families, we didn't have access to a car so my father's brother-in-law Jackie was sent for (I don't think Jackie ever refused help to anyone) and he had the job of transporting us all lock, stock and barrel. The reason we went to Ballyliffin was simple: my father's family had holidayed there for many years when they were all younger and his memories of those days were all happy ones - except for the ghost who frequented one of the houses they holidayed in for many years. Despite many strange happenings, the locals never told them about the ghost until they started taking another house for their holidays!

When I say we all went, I mean Ma, Donna, Kath, Nuala, Kevin, Marian, John Flood, Mammy and Daddy and yours truly, to a two-bedroom cottage at the back of a shop on the main street. Da (probably quite wisely) stayed at home. The craic was great, the laughs plentiful and the days seemed endless. We went to the beach, we went walking, we played cards and we played games. Mammy was great at entertaining us and keeping us happy. If we were happy, she was happy, and happy we were.

This was to be the first of many such holidays we all had together. Even later in life, when we had married and our children had come along, we continued to holiday together and have created many happy memories which no one can ever rob us of as they are locked safely in the vault of our hearts.

Though my aunt Rose had gone to live in England, we still kept in touch on a regular basis. She came home most summers, bringing her family with her. In the early years of her marriage she had three daughters - May, Sandra and Donna – and, later on, they had a son called Peter. I never really got to know him as well as I did the girls because he was born just a few years before my wife Sally and I got married and, by then, I had stopped going over to England on holiday.

I remember the excitement of making that journey (initially by train and boat and then, later, by plane). On the first visit, I went with my aunt Kath and Donna at Christmas time, and I can still recapture the feeling of magic as we made a special journey from Leatherhead up to the big stores in London. I remember the excitement of seeing Santa Claus (the real one) and how overawed I was when he called me by my name. Even though Mammy and Daddy were not there, I didn't feel alone. You see, the love that they showed me was always shown to me by all the others from 97, Lecky Road: after all, I was 'wee Johnny'. The time came when it was decided that Donna and I could make the journey by plane on our own. I was about twelve years old and she was about nine and a half. They all took us to Nutts Corner Airport and saw us on the plane, with instructions not to speak to strangers and all the usual warnings. You'd have thought we were never coming back.

Rose and Peter were to meet us at Heathrow, but as they say, the best-laid plans of mice and men will always go astray. We got there, but they didn't... well, not on time. So, being the bold adventurers we were, into London we did go on the bus; sure, as a man of the world, I knew you could get the Greenline bus to Leatherhead and then take a No 65 to 6, Appledale Road. No bother to Donna and me; off we set. When we arrived there, my aunt Rose was up to high doh, but was so relieved we were safe that she broke down and cried. I loved her more than she ever knew.

We had a great holiday with her. We went to Brighton, and I remember when we reached the cobble beach and saw the crowds, asking myself, *what would it be like if they had our beaches?* We went to the New Forest and saw the ponies. I went to speedway racing, the cricket and the football with Peter; after all, we were men. Like all good things, it came to an end too soon, but the memories are all mine. Many years later, Mammy produced a letter I had written to her during that stay. She had kept it safely, just as she had done with so many other things belonging to us all. She was the original magpie.

Uncle Johnny, by the very nature of things, spent a lot of time working in England, as indeed did a lot of men from Derry back in those days because they couldn't get work at home. Every weekend, Johnny sent a wire, as they called a money order, to help out at home. He came over about twice a year. I remember him being generous to a fault. 'You spoil him rotten whenever you come home,' Mammy used to say to him, and his answer was always the same: 'Sure it's my right. Aren't I his uncle?' I was so much part of them all, even in such a short space of time. When he lived at Lecky Road, Johnny kept greyhounds in the shed in the backyard. Those dogs were treated better than some humans. Again, as I sat at the front door, I would watch Johnny and many other men 'walk the greyhounds', as the saying goes. It helped, I am sure, to fill out an otherwise long day.

He eventually came home, got a job in the then booming BSR factory, met and married a girl from Nelson Street, Kathleen McFadden, and they had six children. They had started married life in the front room of the house in Lecky Road, with my aunt Kath (who had taken over the house when we moved to Creggan) and uncle Jim, along with Donna, Kitsy and young Jim, occupying the rest of the house for a while until Kath and Jim were housed at Cable Street, one of the new houses built nearby. Johnny and Kathleen then took over at No 97, continuing our contact with the people of the area, just as Kath had done before them. Kath, as I mentioned, also made me feel special in the wee things she did for me.

My thoughts have wandered to the Lecky Road again, and when I think of it, I see it as the best community, made up of the most genuine and caring people, one could ever wish to be a part of. Possessions of a material kind were not in abundance, but generosity of heart certainly was. I can't remember, as I grew up, ever seeing a locked door anywhere in the area, from William Street to Hamilton Street, or any of the streets running off it, in what is now referred to as the Bogside. I was chatting to someone recently, who told me that it was the police who would have pulled a door closed as they walked around the area late at night on their tour of duty. Changed times!

One only has to think of the Columban celebrations which happened around June 9th every year to see a community in total action. The men of the area painted the fronts of houses, and enough paint was found to do all of the houses. If someone wasn't able in any particular house to do the painting, others did it for them. The women, meanwhile, were busy making or repairing bunting to be hung across the streets at rooftop level.

The whole Long Tower area ended up a festoon of colour every year at this time. The carnival and the parade were a very big part of this time of festivities, and the floats that came along the Lecky Road out towards the Brandywell area were outstanding. A week or fortnight of activities followed in the Showgrounds, where the usual fairground fun was to be found. Again, I can only recall sunshine and a great buzz around the place; no rain or gloom. Nowadays, when people are asked to do things, the first question that seems to come is, 'what grants are available?' Not so in those days; there was just a willingness to be involved and a lot of heart. All of this was built around St Columba's Day and there was a great sense of us belonging to him and him belonging to us, the pilgrim who came, saw and fell in love with Derry and the oak grove.

Saint Columba's feast day Mass would always be said in those days, in Irish, on June 9th in the Long Tower church. People from all over the city and surrounding areas would come to take part in these celebrations. The Mass would always be followed by the blessing of the water in St Columb's Well. The well is still to be seen in the new Bogside (redevelopment has robbed us of many of the landmarks I remember from then). It was always carefully prepared every year with great pride by Tommy Mitchell; if my memory serves me right, his family has had that privilege for generations. Derry needs, now more than ever, people like the old folk. It was among these people that the seeds of today, and my love of community, were planted, watered and tended with such loving care and example.

Another memory I have is of a journey I made most Friday and Saturday nights with my father. We covered a lot of the streets running off the Lecky Road as we delivered, on foot, the shoes people had left with him to be repaired. I suppose this, in turn, led me to know a lot of people of the area from a very early age. I recall a raincoat he wore, with the lining either cut or torn, so that he could put the shoes inside of the coat, making them easier to carry. A thought that has just come to me is that, in some way, he did the same with us: as children and as adults, he carried us, no matter what the situation we had gotten ourselves into, and never, ever saw us as being too heavy.

Another place where I found total love and acceptance was in the home of my paternal grandparents, Johnny and Mary McCallion, at 15, Beechwood Street. They, like my Ma and Da, never ever indicated to us that we were in any way different from their other grandchildren. The relationship with them was different simply in the sense that it was more 'in and out again' as we only visited them once a week for a few hours. My granny McCallion was a woman who had a soft, round, jolly face, and she was a great baker. There was always plenty of homemade scones, pastry and cakes whenever you went there. My aunt Bridget, also a great baker, was very well taught by the master.

There always seemed to be plenty of children around there, and how could it have been any other way? Kathleen Devine, my aunt Annie's daughter, lived there. My aunt Maggie had three children: Lily, Neil and John. My aunt Lizzie had two daughters, Margaret and Bridie, and if that wasn't enough, my uncle Tommy and aunt Mary had I don't know how many children! So, as I said, it was always a full house but a happy house. In the midst of all of them (and very much part of the family and loved by all) was Mary Ann (McGilloway), who had reared my father and his sisters and brothers while their parents went out to work. She never left the family home, even after the children did, becoming a much-loved and respected member of the family. Many tears were shed when she died.

It was this side of the family where I first came across death (though, at the time, I never really took its meaning in). I can remember my father's youngest sister, Theresa, dying at a very young age, and then my aunt Annie died; both of tuberculosis, which was rife in Derry at the time. My granda McCallion was next to go, and my memory of that time was of my father sitting up at night to help care for his father and still going to work the next day. He had to; no one else could do his job. My granny McCallion took diabetes and later developed gangrene in her foot; the doctors wanted to amputate her leg but the family said no. Amazingly, when she died, there wasn't a trace of the gangrene. *How they must have prayed,* I thought - the mind of the child at play again.

She died on June 29th, 1958, and was buried on the day Sweden played Brazil in the final of the World Cup. The only TV within the family circle at that time was in her house in Beechwood Street, so we had to miss it (though I recently discovered that some of the elders of the family did, in fact, watch it in an upstairs room after the funeral was over).

It wasn't all doom and gloom back then, though; there were many happy times as well. Christmas was always very special, and even now I still try to make a point of visiting Beechwood Street, if not on Christmas Day then on Boxing Day (though Covid has affected that this past few years, unfortunately). I can also remember my aunt Bridget getting married to Jackie Cooley. They had their wedding breakfast in the house (again, I don't know how they did it) and in the afternoon, the nephews and nieces joined in the celebration. Of all my father's sisters, I have a very special place in my heart for Bridget.

My aunt Kath was a lady extraordinaire: solid, reliable and, most of all, loveable. I have left her to the last, not because she is the least of my people but because, apart from my Ma and Da in my earlier years and outside of Mammy and Daddy, she is the one who made the biggest impact on my life at that time. Kath, because of circumstances, was a forerunner of today's independent or liberated woman, inasmuch as she was a mainstay of support for her family. Jim, her husband, had to work in England. As a married man, he wouldn't have wanted to be away from home but in those days jobs were hard to come by in Derry. So Kath did her bit by running 'the clubs', as they say in Derry.

This was a method by which a person would get a docket to buy goods in a designated shop, up to a certain amount as indicated on the docket. It was then up to Kath, as the club holder, to collect a certain amount from that person each week. She had built up quite a run over the years, and on many a Friday night (or Saturday during the day) I would escort her - or even go on my own, sometimes - to certain homes throughout the area to collect these payments. Then, on the Monday or Tuesday following, she would go around the different shops and pay in her money. In turn, she was paid an agreed amount of commission on her returns.

So that was the Kath who worked to help support her family. I know that people thought she had money, but I believe she got no more or no less than she deserved. I spent many Saturday nights with Kath and her family and loved nothing better than getting up for nine o'clock Mass on a Sunday, in the Long Tower Chapel, and coming down to the house afterwards. Kath always made you a big fry; nearly as big as her heart, but not quite.

During my time at St Columb's College, I would have gone to Kath's for my dinner, and I suppose we became even closer then. It was then that I would pick her brains about things Mammy wouldn't or didn't want to talk about regarding my life story. At one stage, before he passed, I was talking to our Kevin about all that was going on in my life and he said that someone said our Mammy should be on tape because she totally believed that we were hers naturally. And guess what? We were and we are, as far as I'm concerned.

Anyway, it was Kath who, when we were talking in later years, told me that the story of my first encounter with Mammy and Daddy was not some fairytale they had made up for my benefit (which is what I thought), but was, in fact, true. This was to be confirmed years later by someone totally unconnected to us. Kath was also the first person to talk to me about a God of love, forgiveness and compassion, and would continually do so whenever we met. She would even invite me to come and find out for myself at charismatic meetings. To which I would say: 'I'm okay, Kath, and it's great for you, but it has to be at a time when I choose to go and see for myself.'

After all, you can take a horse to water, but you can't make it drink until it is ready. I have many memories of this great lady that are mine to keep and cherish, just as the love she showered on me sustains me and reassures me in times of need.

Another branch of the wider family connection is a group we affectionately refer to as 'the Dohertys'. They are the family of the late Joe and Cassie Doherty. Cassie was better known to us as Cassie Diver. She was a cousin of Mammy's but more like a sister, as her father was killed in the First World War (either before or just after she was born). She spent most of her younger years in the home of my Ma and Da so that her mother, Maryann Diver, could work in the factory to support them both. There were no great state benefits back then for the widows and orphans of the many men who had been killed in that war. We spent a lot of time with the Dohertys, and I guarantee you that anyone who visited their house felt better as they left. I was (and remain) very good friends with their daughter, Marie - who is older than me, a fact I am sure she would want me to point out! To her and the others, I say, 'thank you'.

Now, because of the very special people about whom I am about to talk, comes one of the most emotional eras of my life to recall. They are the three people who, apart from Mammy and Daddy, played the biggest role in giving me stability in my younger life and (along with Sally and the wains) the security of love in my later years. I am, of course, referring to my sisters and brother: Nuala, Marian and Kevin.

I suppose, by the very nature of things, we drift along in our childhood, not really aware of life's little tricks and turns. We were brothers and sisters, family and clan. Like any other family, we must have had our ups and downs, but I honestly can't recall them. As I said, Mammy and Daddy cloaked us in love. All of our childhood together was spent at 24, Inishowen Gardens, in total love and security.

Nuala and Marian both went to St Mary's Intermediate School after primary school. Because of the age gaps between us, I suppose we were poles apart in things like shared interests and friends. But the seeds of love were being firmly planted by two of God's greatest gardeners that I have ever met in my lifetime: Mammy and Daddy.

Kevin went to Rosemount Boys' and then on to St Columb's College. Unlike me, Kevin was the natural academic; the brute didn't even have to do that much studying to succeed at school. I honestly believe (and I know I joked with Kevin about it), when he was made vice principal of his school, that he had come by the road that many of his pupils would try to travel today, but that because of his own experiences he would always be one step ahead of them.

It was really only in later years that the foundations laid by Mammy and Daddy were seen to be so solid. If you really want to know what we think of each other (and I am sure that I speak for the others when I say this), just try and cross us, or say something about us, and you will find out just how deep our love for each other really is. Nuala stayed at home longer than the rest of us, and I know a lot of it had to do with her love for Mammy and Daddy. If you think I love them deeply, you should meet Nuala. In 1976, she finally married the fella she had met in the late '60s: Michael Kolczak. They now have a fine son; John Edward, my nephew. Nuala, to me, was the original Martha; always running around, doing for and giving to people, all of her life. Even today, she still manages to continue giving. She is the most generous lady.

Marian is 'the wain' (and she will always be our wain). She would give the impression of having this world all sorted out, but I just wonder. Someday, I must find out for myself. There is almost a ten-year gap in age between us but none in our love. Marian was growing up in our midst at a time when we were going through our self-interested teenage years, and then, during the years that we were settling down to married life, she herself was going through those same teenage years.

I suppose, like all big brothers, I was very protective of her and would have done anything to stop her from getting hurt. As she grew older, Derry was no longer to be part of Marian's everyday life; when she was in her early twenties, she headed off to England. I don't think that any of us for a moment thought she would stay, but stay she did. She, too, married a fella called Michael (Joyce is his surname) and they went on to have three fine sons: Mark, Kevin and Simon.

Now to the big one (in more ways than one): my wee brother Kevin. All six foot three-and-a-quarter inches of him. I suppose, in many ways, Kevin benefited from my mistakes. Maybe, at the time, he hated me for it, but because of the nearly six-year age gap, I had already made the errors that he was willing to make all over again. So, to college he did go, and there he did stay until that part of his education was complete.

He won a place for himself at Da La Salle teacher training college in Manchester; my mother and father were both over the moon, and deservedly so. Kevin was the first of us to leave home and go abroad. It was a big wrench to us all, as we felt we were losing him a bit (I should say that, by this time, I had also moved away from Inishowen Gardens... all 200 yards away to my new wife Sally's family home in Malin Gardens!).

No sooner had he arrived in Manchester than Mammy arrived over to our house 'in a whole state', as we would say in Derry. Kevin wanted to come home again; he hated the place and was so unhappy. She had to phone him at a certain time, and would I talk to him? I believe if I hadn't been strong that night, Kevin's life would have taken a different course. Putting it simply, Mammy would have given in to him and he would have come home then.

But he didn't, and by all accounts, he actually enjoyed Manchester, because he told many tales of his time there. Kevin, in his turn, went the way of the rest of us and married the girl of his childhood years, Carmel McCafferty, and they had a family of one girl, Muire, and two sons, Brendan and Cormac.

It was within the network of this family that I grew up and found the love that would sustain me throughout my life, and I am glad; I wouldn't have had it any other way.

The Growing Years

My parents' lives had been given willingly to serve and care for others. They moved to Creggan so that they could look after my Ma and Da as well as for us as we came along, one by one. In the late fifties, Da became ill with dementia. I suppose Mammy knew he wasn't going to get better, so she prayed that he be released from his suffering. To gain this release for him, she - wait for it - did a deal with God.

Her brother Alec had been in hospital for about fifteen years at that time. He had fought in the Second World War and came back suffering from shell shock. He never got back to himself and the doctors said he would never be at home again. So Mammy prayed to God, promising him, in return for ending her father's suffering, He could send Alec home to them, where they would care for him for as long as they were able. And that was her deal with the man above. Amazingly, he answered her prayers; within five months of Da's death, Uncle Alec came home to stay with them, and there he stayed, for 21 years, until his death on November 12th, 1982 (just nine days later, we had another loss when Con, the brother of Mary McLaughlin and a good friend of mine since our schooldays, also passed away).

If God kept his part of the bargain, Mammy and Daddy certainly kept theirs, caring for Alec right up to the very end. Even as they did this, their children were never neglected, nor, later, their grandchildren. But I will speak of that later.

In 1954, I sat and passed the 11-plus (how happy Mammy and Daddy were) and so to St Columb's College the boy did go. I spent three years there and probably struggled during most of that time, truth be told. A friend suggested that, if I got a job in the old BSR factory he would help me get a trade. I decided to go for it (Mammy would often tell of how she cried when I went to work that first morning). I was the manly age of 14 years and eight months old, stepping out into the big world with all of its knocks and bumps and full of great plans for the life ahead.

When the first big knock of my young, protected life arrived - the death of my Da on January 17th, 1960 - it was traumatic, to say the least. The second big disappointment hit just a few months later; there was a load of layoffs at the BSR factory, so there went the apprenticeship out the window. I was now beginning to live in the real world, with all of its knocks and disappointments - and, even, broken dreams.

It was shortly after this that I started to work in Paddy Bannon's menswear shop, in Butcher Street, under the guidance of two men who were later to become very special friends of mine. Donald ('Don' as he was known to many, but always 'Donald' to me) O'Doherty and big Tony McGeehan helped mould me into the professional salesman that I became. No university course could ever have prepared me for working life as well as they did.

I was also enjoying my social life to the full, running to the Corinthian dance hall on Friday nights to participate in ballroom dancing, the Lourdes hall for the céilí on a Saturday night and then up the town most other nights.

I remember the day at work when Donald said his wife Mary (McLaughlin) would like me to call down to her Irish dancing class because she was looking for fellas for a team. *Nothing ventured, nothing gained,* I thought, and sure I could dance as well as anyone on a Saturday night at the céilí. Foolish me! I remember the embarrassment of learning how to do 'one-two-threes' and 'sevens' properly as all of those trained dancers looked on.

But something more important was taking place in my life: the forging of new friendships, with many of them becoming long-lasting ones. I went to many parts of the country with the McLaughlin School of Dancing and was in many winning teams. For me, the pinnacle was being part of the first McLaughlin team to win the All-Ireland twelves competition at the new composed dance championships, held in the Mansion House in Dublin, in 1963. And we went back the following year and won it again.

We also went on tour to Boston, Chicago and Minneapolis in March of 1965; an experience I will never forget. In the midst of all of this, other, more important, things were happening. Although we didn't realise it at the time, our characters were being moulded: our self-esteem was being built up and our confidence was being boosted, therefore helping us to take our place in the world.

Running alongside all of this was the age-old 'boy/girl' pursuit; in love one day and hating each other the next. My friends at this time consisted mainly of Con McLaughlin, a friend from my schooldays at the Rosemount Boys', Barry Doherty, who lived just two doors from my home in Creggan, Don Lynch from Demesne Avenue and John Flood, who I mentioned earlier. We five spent our teenage years running around together. As I said, girls dominated the scene at this time of our lives. I forget how many times I thought I was in love and that 'this is it'. My only problem was that a very special friend had drifted into my life around then. I can remember the first time I saw her at a céilí in the Old Ritz dance hall; it was there I gave her the first of what was to be many dances between the two of us. Sally Quigley was her name.

I used to tell her of the girls I loved and ask for her advice, but at the back of my mind, even then, I used to wonder how they would accept my friendship with Sally; because I wasn't breaking it for anyone. She was my best friend. My mother was always saying to me how nice a girl Sally was, and she was Kitty Mellon's daughter, one of Mammy's best friends from her youth. We tend to refer to people a lot in Derry by their maiden names, and the Stephen Quigley who I referred to earlier was her father. So I guess you could say that the die was cast, as they say, and I didn't even see it.

I looked far and wide for this girl of my dreams and told Sally all about my escapades. During my friendship time with Sally, we did go out on a few dates, but I always had this fear that if it developed into anything deeper we would end up fighting and falling out, and ultimately going our separate ways. Also, I could go in and out quite freely to Sally's home as her friend, whereas any fella she went out with on a date was never allowed near the house.

She used to go as far as the chemist on Beechwood Avenue with whoever was leaving her home, where I would 'happen' to come along after I had left home whichever girl I thought I loved at that time. We would say goodnight to whoever Sally was with and head on up to her house. It was a good set-up we had: why complicate it all by going out?

But the pull I had to her was becoming harder to ignore so I finally decided to take the plunge. On our very first official date, I arrived at the appointed time, was greeted at the door by Sally's father and shown into the living room, where Mrs Quigley was sitting. We talked about whatever seemed to be appropriate to talk about at the time until Sally came downstairs, ready to go to the pictures. We said we would be back at a certain time (Sally's mother wanted all details confirmed).

We got ready to go. The bold boy Johnny was not a bit nervous (at least, not so they could see or sense) until it came to the time to bid my farewells. 'See you later, Mrs Mellon,' says I, using Mrs Quigley's maiden name. It gave them something to laugh about for years. By this time she was terminally ill, but I never remember her complaining; in fact, she laughed right to the end. She loved a cigarette and said to Mr Quigley just before she died, 'Give us a fag for the road, Stephen'.

Then Sally and I fell out. I can't remember what it was that we argued about, exactly, but looking back, I think at the root of it was that I was dragging my heels with her a wee bit and she was losing patience with me. At the time, her mother was quite ill in hospital and I wanted to go over to see her, but I couldn't because of this rift. Then, one Friday night, I went to a céilí in Strabane. I saw Sally walk in the door with her friend and the penny finally dropped... she was everything to me. I missed her. I told Barry that night that I was going to go off with Sally and that I was going to marry her.

As a result of reconciling with Sally, I was then able to go and see Mrs Quigley at the hospital. I didn't realise how ill she was and I will never forget my entrance into her ward. She was in a single ward and the whole family connection had gathered in it. As I entered, someone (Sally, I think) said, 'There's Johnny', and, as only she could do in her own inimitable style, Mrs Quigley said, 'Ah, lovely Johnny'. I think I blushed to my roots (I was to find out later that this was her way of teasing Sally when she mentioned my name).

I now know that one of the main reasons I resisted going with Sally was simply the fear that our special friendship would go the way the others had gone - downhill - and I didn't want that.

Life was again on the up and up for me, but it was about to take a terrible turn downwards for Sally. Her mother died the following week, leaving her to care for her father and her brothers Stephen, Tommy and Michael. I remember her great sadness at this time and I could only imagine her pain and sense of great loss. But Sally is one of those people who is able to pick herself up, dust herself down and then get on with life. Our courtship continued, and, as I mentioned earlier, Sally's father Stephen Quigley was to play a big part in making me the person I am today. I believe that because of this man's great example of caring for others (despite his own illnesses), I became less selfish and more tolerant of others. He was never, in the years that I knew him, in good health; he suffered from chest, heart and lung problems but was always ready to care for others and laugh at life. How spoiled I had been, growing up with my slight asthma attacks, compared to this man's health problem.

As time moved on, we became close friends (at least I hope he saw it that way) and I was proud to call him 'Mr Q'. He asked me to call him Stephen, but I couldn't; I respected him too much.

This, then, was another special time of my life as we planned for the future and drifted into the idea of getting married. Sally and I got engaged by the side of her mother's grave on November 21st, 1963. Earlier that day, I had taken the ring to show it to Mr Q, who was in hospital again, and I suppose that was my way of asking for Sally's hand in marriage. Incidentally, as we were sitting with him the following evening in the hospital, the news came through that President Kennedy had been shot dead.

During those years, many friendships were made, but a few, in particular, were to deepen as the years rolled by. Sally and Connie Glackin, neighbours of the Quigleys in Malin Gardens, offered great guidance and help to us throughout the years. Also, Donald and Mary O'Doherty (she of the McLaughlin School of Irish Dancing fame), whose house was my harbour if a storm was blowing and the place where I spent most of my Tuesday nights over the years. I met many wonderful people through my involvement in Irish dancing but found a particularly special friend and confidant in Anna McLaughlin, who I could always go to for advice and a listening ear, sure in the knowledge that whatever I shared with her would stay with her. She had such a gentle manner and I always took on board the sound advice she gave.

So here I was; a young man, barely into his twenties, and already blessed with a loving family, close friends and a woman who was everything to me; I was so excited about what the future had in store.

Companions On A Journey

The date and place were set for our marriage: August 30th, 1965, in St Mary's Church, Creggan. Like any young couple, we had our dreams and aspirations and couldn't see anything that would stop us from fulfilling them. But, as we planned for the future, the past was to move in on Mammy when, for some unknown reason, someone told her I would have to be married as Kelly and not McCallion. Despite the fact that I had been legally adopted, she believed them. It was around then that I started to sense her fears again. I tried to reassure her of how my love for her couldn't be taken away from her by anyone; not even the woman who was listed as 'mother' on my birth certificate - Rose Kelly. I suppose it may have been around this time that I started to wonder about Rose. But any move to find out about her would have upset my Mammy too much so I put her to the back of my mind again.

Sally and I got married and moved into her family home. She had to 'watch' her father, as we say, because of Stephen's ill health. Even before we married, we had become a team of three and it was only natural that it should stay this way. We were very happy. We had each other and we had the support from our families which gave us the security on which to build our new life. Shortly after getting married, Sally fell pregnant, and so we had to plan for the arrival of our first child. The excitement was great; wasn't this what we'd hoped for? The first of the children we said we wanted was on his or her way. As we waited for the birth, not knowing if it was a boy or a girl, we wondered who it would resemble, and I used to laugh and joke about the unknown. Sure we didn't know what Rose Kelly looked like, nor did we know anything about my natural father.

That's how it worked; she would come creeping into our lives and out again. I was always very open about the fact I'd been adopted and couldn't understand others in my position who seemed to find it such a problem. Sure wasn't I so blessed by the mother and father who had chosen me as their son, and the love and care they showered me with? I suppose I assumed everyone else felt as secure as I did.

On May 20th, 1966, Edward Pearse McCallion was born. He was almost six weeks premature and weighed 5lb 4oz. I remember the first time I saw him. The nurse lifted him from his cot and held him up for me to look at through a glass window; her hands covered most of his body. He was so small but so perfect. It was to be almost three weeks before we were allowed to take him home and cuddle him ourselves. On that day, our world seemed to be so perfect. Our plan was coming together.

Not long after this, we found Sally was pregnant again, and we awaited this birth with the same anticipation. Sadly, it was during this time that Mr Quigley's health took a turn for the worse; he seemed to be in and out of hospital more often. He just loved nursing Edward and helping Sally in any way possible. Slowly but surely, however, even the small things started to become impossible for him. I know this hurt him deeply. To me, Stephen Quigley was the joker; not father, father-in-law or friend, just out and out joker.

Edward was about nine months old and hadn't cut a tooth. Sally was very worried and asked her father what she should do. He advised her to make an appointment with the dentist and take Edward along to have his gums scraped. Sally did what he suggested and set off with Edward on the day of the appointment. Did Mr Q stop her? No. Down the street she went, baby in pram. Did he call her back? No. Sally arrived at the surgery and told the dentist why she was there. He went into fits of laughter and couldn't believe it was her father who had sent her down. Did Mr Quigley say that he was sorry on their return? No. He just laughed his head off. She trusted him so much he could have told her anything and she would have believed him. What a man.

As the time for the second arrival came near, Sally was nursing her father more and more. She never complained and was always willing to help him, no matter how she may have felt herself. Nothing was too much when it came to her father. It was during this time that I really started to become aware of her great strengths. I found myself falling deeper and deeper in love with her. Before this, I thought that I knew all about love, but I didn't. I had never been asked in my life to show love as Sally was doing; serving others and expecting nothing in return. I always knew of her love for Mr Quigley but never really realised how deep it was until then.

On Thursday, April 6th, 1967, Mr Quigley was admitted to hospital, and it was during that night that our second baby started to arrive; again, early, by all calculations. On April 7th, Stephen McCallion was born. On April 11th, Sally's daddy passed away, never having seen the new baby. He had gone into a coma and deteriorated rapidly and the hospital organised an ambulance to take Sally to see him. She went on April 10th and stayed with him for one hour; it was all they would allow her. During this time he regained consciousness. He wasn't able to speak, but opened his eyes and turned his head to her. Even yet, I can remember and feel the pain of that time, and thinking, how can I ever replace this man in her life? I now know that I never could, and that's the way it is; even today. He has his place in her heart and I have mine. Our own son Stephen would often ask, 'Why have I only one Christian name and the others have two?'

Our answer was simple: 'We couldn't have given you any other name, and if you turn out to be half the man of your granda then we will be proud of you.'

When I think of it, my Ma was a character in her own right, too. She used to go to her room and smoke her clay pipe, which she filled with twist tobacco from her half ounce that she got twice a week. No one was to know of this vice despite the smell it left around the house for hours afterwards. The funniest story I remember of her was her total innocence when it came to modern technology. Mammy had gone and bought our first TV from Paddy Coyle's in the Diamond. The set arrived and was placed in the allocated spot in the living room to await the five o'clock switch-on time of the first programme of the day. We waited. Then someone asked where my Ma was; just as they did, she arrived in the room wearing her Sunday best apron, her hair neatly back in her own style (we often told her that the granny in *The Beverly Hillbillies* copied her hairstyle). Mammy asked her where she was going.

'Nowhere', came the reply.

'So why are you dressed up, Ma?'

'If you lot think I am going to sit here in my auld disabelles (an old Derry slang word for clothes) and let that crowd in the TV look out at me like that, you have another thing coming to you.'

Just as others passed on, so did my Ma; quite suddenly, on May 1st, 1968, just three days after our third son, Emmet, had been born. It was another loss that affected us all profoundly, but no one as much as Mammy. She was devastated, and I don't know if she ever really came to terms with my Ma's death.

Another two years rolled by and then Catherine was born on July 20th, 1970. She was the little girl Sally had always dreamed of. Just before Catherine was born, I started a new job as manager of the Whitehaven Furnishing Co in Bishop Street. The owner, Mr Mullane, was to become not just an employer but, along with his wife Nancy, a very good friend. He was the first to plant the seed of us buying our own home. I would laugh at him time and again, but buy we did; in July, 1971, we moved to Danesfort Crescent. With it being the early seventies, the Troubles were a big part of life in Derry, but despite this, we were full of life's hopes and dreams. The children were growing and Sally had decided to go back to university and do a teacher training course in Coleraine, travelling daily. Everything was perfect in our world.

But then, on September 3rd, 1973, that perfect world was turned upside down. We had just returned from holidays and the children had gone back to school that Monday morning. By that evening, everything was in turmoil. The boys were out looking for chestnuts with their friends and Emmet had decided to go out on his bike to find them. But he lost control of it and was hit by a car. Some young men, along with a Mrs Gilmartin, took him in the back of their car to hospital; we are forever in their debt. Sally was in a panic trying to trace me, thinking I was out on calls selling carpets, but it turned out I was just around the corner in a neighbour's home, oblivious to all that was unfolding, when she found me.

The journey to the hospital felt like a lifetime. There were checkpoints all over the place because of the Troubles, delaying us even more. I became so angry with God. Who could let this happen to a five-year-old child who had never done anything wrong? I felt, if I had done something, it should be me lying there; not our little boy. Emmet had sustained a bad head injury and was in intensive care for almost three weeks. During this time, we had several very anxious moments and I became more and more angry with God. But Sally never wavered in her belief that he would be alright. Again, this was the inner strength that is so much a fabric of her being.

Emmet did get better, slowly at first and then in leaps and bounds. But as he got better, my anger with God intensified. *Nobody will ever have control of my life again; I will do it on my own,* I vowed to myself. All I needed was Sally and the wains and all at 24 Inishowen Gardens. I didn't even need Rose Kelly; sure, I didn't even know her.

It really is at a time of crisis that you get to know who your real friends are, and if we didn't already know before Emmet's accident, well, we certainly did afterwards. We owe a great debt of gratitude to everyone within our family circle, but in particular to Mammy and Daddy. They completely took over the caring of Edward, Stephen and Catherine by coming to our home and making them as secure as possible, giving us the freedom to be with Emmet night and day at the hospital. Among the wider circle of friends who offered words of support and comfort were the many neighbours who called to ask Mammy how Emmet and we were doing. Fr Jim McGonagle, a good friend of ours, cut short his holidays and returned to Derry to help in whatever way he could. We will never forget that.

In later years, a friend once remarked to me that we could have many acquaintances but few true friends in life: if that be so, then we had all of ours surrounding us at that time. I can't think of this time without thinking of two special people (and I don't think I ever told them this) who provided a haven for me in the midst of turmoil. Whenever I called with them first thing in the morning (on my way home from the hospital to see the children), they made me my breakfast despite the fact they were getting ready to go to work themselves. Nothing was ever a bother to them. True friends never look for anything in return, and they didn't: Patricia and David Noble. Patricia, sadly, is no longer with us, but I will never forget the hand of friendship both she and David extended towards me.

Up until this time, my faith had played a big part in my life, but after what happened to Emmet, I couldn't care less. Sometimes I would just go through the motions because, as Sally said, the wains were at an impressionable age. I hung in there, for her, but in my heart, during those next few years, God wasn't anywhere in my plans; I had taken control and the ship was on a course that I, myself, had set.

We moved house, in 1977, to Aberfoyle Crescent. It was all part of this plan of ours. Another move in 1979 took us to Juniper Park in Foyle Springs; the home we have lived in to this day. For a few years before this, Sally had been hinting that we should have another child before it was too late. She had graduated and was now teaching in the Long Tower Girls' School. But no one was ever going to have control of my heartstrings again, remember? So, no more children for me.

In the seventies, someone decided to hold a Mass of thanksgiving for adopted children and their parents. I thought it was a brilliant idea so I approached Kevin, Nuala and Marian so that we could ask Mammy and Daddy to go to the Mass with us. When Kevin and I eventually brought the matter up with her, Mammy asked, 'Why would we want to go?' I really believe she felt it wasn't for us. It was only when we said we would be proud to be there with them at our sides that she finally gave in. After a beautiful Mass celebrated by Bishop Daly in the Nazareth House chapel, we were all invited to have a cup of tea and a chat in the hall. During this time, I met a friend of mine who had adopted a son and she told me she had been speaking to my mother, saying to her how nice the whole idea was when Mammy replied, 'It was a lovely idea for you and yours'. I say this to give an insight into my mother's way of thinking. We were hers and that was that; she did not see us as adopted.

In September 1979, Pope John Paul II made his now historic visit to Ireland, and, believe me, if he had been in my back garden I wouldn't have turned my head around to see him. The years had left me bitter. Emmet's scars had healed, but mine hadn't. His could be seen, while mine were out of sight. Sally said that even if I didn't go to Drogheda, she would take the children herself. I said that suited me fine, and it did. Then I started thinking, *what if anything were to happen, and us so far apart?* I knew then that I had to go to be close to them, just in case. Sally travelled with Patricia McDaid, her friend of many years (and one of mine from the dancing days). She had Catherine with her and I took the boys and Sally's cousin, Damien Quigley, in our car. There was a great sense of expectancy in the air that Saturday morning, with all roads leading from the North to Dublin or Drogheda. The excitement mounted.

It was like one of those lovely days that I could remember from my childhood, when we all made our way to Buncrana shore, brought a picnic and played on the beach; that was the kind of atmosphere that prevailed. The time was fast approaching to herald the arrival of John Paul II. I looked around me: I couldn't believe that people could be this hyped up over any man. But they were! The helicopter escort appeared first and the cheers went up, then the word spread that it was not him so it died down again. I remember thinking, *what is he going to see as he flies overhead?* And, of all the things that came into my head, the one that stands out the most is, *the toilets have no roofs; that will be some sight for him.*

Suddenly, the crowd went wild. He was overhead and fast approaching the touchdown area. Then followed the motorcade, with all eyes on the Popemobile. He made his way to the specially-built altar to concelebrate Mass with the many priests who had gathered here. Nothing I had seen or heard so far had changed my mind from its set way.

That is, until the homily, when he uttered an appeal to the men of violence to lay down their arms. At that moment, I am sure everyone in that field heard him speak to the gunmen. Everyone except me, that is. I felt as if he was speaking directly to me, because, with my non-involvement and my continued resistance to any of its teachings, and by generally not living by the teachings of Christ, I was a man of violence against his church.

I felt a great weight lift away from me, and I knew I could trust Him again. I came away from there that day knowing there would be another child, and that I could, and would, take the risk to love again. On July 19th, 1980, Mary was born. Our joy was complete. She was (and still is) the icing on the cake.

Living In The Real World

We were all at Mass in St. Eugene's Cathedral one Sunday (Mary was about two years old) and, at that time, we were like nomads when it came to going to Mass. We were equal distance, roughly, from about three or four churches, but none of them really felt like home to us. So that particular week, it was the cathedral. Anyway, on leaving Mass, Fr Kieran O'Doherty was out in the church grounds and called me aside as he wanted to ask me to do something. Did I know that the new Holy Family church would be opening out our way in September 1983, and could I organise the stewards for that occasion?

I had never really gotten involved with any aspect of parish life before; it was always the cliques (or 'clicks', as we say in Derry) doing all that sort of stuff. So I thought I would take this opportunity to make my point.

Being the diplomat that I am, I said: 'Father, you have a golden opportunity to do away with the cliques and involve the ordinary people.'

I will never forget his reply: 'Johnny, in ten years' time, the people who help out now will still be helping out then, because that's the way things are - more's the pity - and they will still be called cliques.'

He was right, I am sorry to say. But I got involved; more and more so as the parish grew.

It was around this time that Sally and I were to add another special friend (to our list of many) in the shape of the young curate appointed to the Holy Family parish that year: Fr Peter Madden. He has since moved on in his ministry, but never, we pray, out of our hearts.

At this stage, I should give an idea of how central Mammy and Daddy were to the rearing of our children. As we say in Derry, they had them spoilt rotten over the years. But it was so much deeper than that. When the children came along in the beginning, Sally was at home caring for them, but just before Catherine was born she started to do a bit of substitute teaching.

Eventually, after a few years, one principal who she worked for in this way challenged her to go and do a teaching degree so that she could teach full-time. Sally is eternally grateful to the late Bill Sharkey, as it was he who gave her the encouragement and confidence in her own ability to do so. This decision meant Sally had to travel on a daily basis to Coleraine; without my mother's willingness to watch the children after school until I finished work, it would not have been possible.

The children grew so close to her and my father during these years. For the first year or so of Sally's course, Catherine wasn't at school, so they had her on a daily basis, from early morning to late at night. I have no doubt that the love Mammy and Daddy showed the children would have more than made up for anything that our absence may have caused. When we realised that Mary was on the way, we didn't know what to do about a childminder, as Mammy wasn't keeping very well at the time.

For some reason, she was depressed and generally listless. Eventually, when we broached the subject and said we were going to get someone to care for the baby while Sally was at work, Mammy nearly had a fit. 'I will watch the new baby whenever it arrives,' she said, and she did - with such love and care as always. Mammy's depression eventually lifted and she used to joke that God had sent Mary to her at the right time. At times I wonder. You see, she was doing what she did best again; caring for others.

Throughout all of these years, from the late 1960s to the mid-1980s, our four older children were growing up and claiming their own space within our hearts. Like any other family, we experienced our fair share of broken dreams, as well as much love and joy, together. I suppose, when it comes to joy and brokenness, they each could tell their own story if and when the time is right for them. But, just to give an insight, I would like to share a few of ours. I said previously that, as young newlyweds, we felt we had it all worked out; the way we planned it is the way we expected it would be. But we hadn't reckoned on our children having their own dreams and wanting to live them out, and live them they did.

Edward had met a young girl and their plan was to go to university in Dublin. Being a year ahead of her at school, he set off to UCD to do an arts degree; we were so proud of him. The following year, however, things started to go wrong for them, and to this day I don't think we ever really got to the bottom of it all. Anyway, he had more or less dropped out without telling us and was, in his own way, coping with the situation. Eventually, he came home and started back on the road to rebuilding his life, as he saw it. And what a fine life he built.

Stephen was the worker who was always going to succeed because he was so determined. He was also the greatest 'homebird' I have ever met, so when he went to St Mary's teacher training college in Belfast for three years we thought the experience would give him a whole new view of life. Did it? No way! He never spent one minute more away from us than he had to during that time.

Since he was young, Emmet had set his mind on being a priest and was quite resolute in his pursuit of this dream. I remember the day he went for his interview. Stephen and Mary drew a poster of him driving a car with a figure of the bishop standing in the middle of the road. The caption read, Don't let anyone stand in your way, Emmet. This was how the family saw it then.

Catherine is my princess; my chatterbox. I could write a book on her alone. But somehow, I feel she will someday write one herself and it will be worth reading. Anyway, like the rest of us, she has had her ups and downs, disappointments and maybe even revelations of a greater love than ever we can show her. I recall her disappointment at not getting the A-level grades she wanted, her determination and resolve to succeed the next year and her delight when she did (by the way, most young people would have been very happy with the marks she achieved the first time around; but that's Catherine).

So off to Queen's to study law she went; this one was going to fulfil our plan. She took ill at the start of her third year and had to drop out for a while. She returned the following year and then, about three months before her finals, she dropped the bombshell that she wanted to drop out again. She had phoned me from Dublin on her way from Cork (where her boyfriend Pat, who she met on her very first day at Queen's, was from) to Belfast, and all I could think was that she needed to get home as quickly as possible.

She arrived that evening, and I thank God she did because what we found was a young person who was on the verge of breaking down mentally with all the pressures she felt - and indeed was applying to herself. As difficult as this was for her, I only know she is a happier and more fulfilled person today. As I said, I could write a book on Catherine alone, never mind the others

So onwards we journeyed along the road of life. My ambition, at this time, was to open my own business - a furniture and carpet shop - and this I did, in November 1985. But within a short space of time, it had turned into a nightmare and I didn't know where to turn. Eventually, I had to close the shop and sell Sally the house so that we could pay off the debts which had built up over this venture. Once more, I wasn't happy with God; He had let me down again. Sally's faith came to the fore as usual, as she insisted that He would see us right in the end. And so began two years of trying to make ends meet - not very successfully, I might add - until I started a job as an area sales representative for a local oil company in September 1989. Things seemed to be on the turn.

But soon afterwards, we had a rude awakening. We had gone on holiday and returned home to find that, while we had been away, our son Stephen and three of his friends had gone out for the day around Donegal, where one of his friends, Brian Hegarty, had fallen down a cliffside. He died in Stephen's arms. We watched Stephen closely for any signs of stress. Thank God, he knew God, in his own way, through the Search youth group. I decided to pay back the group some of what I felt we owed them in the only way I knew: by giving my time and energy to help out whenever, and however, I was needed. Before going there, I decided to do a Cursillo weekend to help me in my preparation to work with our young people. Cursillo is a global movement whose primary purpose is to encourage practising Christians to renew and strengthen their love of Jesus. I had resisted many approaches made to me by others who wanted me to do this weekend over the past few years, but I felt now was the right time.

Up to this point, the children had been making their own way in life and all seemed to be going well until this tragedy struck us (though it was nothing near to how it had struck Brian's family). I didn't go on the weekend to be part of Cursillo, really; it was to be part of Search. It was on that weekend that I had my strangest encounter with Rose Kelly to date.

The speaker, Sr Susan Evangelist, was trying to explain that we shouldn't fear life after death and used an example of a story of twins being born. In a strange way, I shot back to the womb of the mother that I never really knew; 'flashback' may have been the proper term. So Rose Kelly touched in again.

That night, I had what I now believe to have been a personal encounter with Christ, because alone in that room I started to reflect on the people I had met in this place and their love for this God and His love for them. I remember thinking how alone I felt among all of them and how I would love to just have Sally here to talk to and for her to listen to me like she always did. I wanted to tell her of this God I was hearing about but couldn't identify with, as I didn't know Him. So I decided to write her a letter; just as if I was talking to her face to face. I started by looking back on my life and trying to identify the times God had been present in my life: as a child in the womb (Rose Kelly again); as I came along that corridor in Nazareth House with Sr Teresa towards the people He had chosen to be my parents; as I grew up at home with Mammy and Daddy, my Ma and Da and uncles and aunts and my sisters and brother; as I dallied through my youth with Sally by my side.

From there, I started to identify Him in the differing personalities of our children: Edward, the laughing Christ; Stephen, the serious but giving Christ; Emmet, the spiritual Christ; Catherine, the Mother Christ (bringing to mind the link with my past in the unexplained actions or habits of Rose) and (last but not least) the child of Christ's love for us: Mary. At that moment, the penny dropped: everything I was looking for here was actually at home, in the form of Sally. She, who had been all of those things to me for so long and who I had taken for granted. *In her lives the Christ I have been searching for,* I thought, elatedly.

A few days later, and still in a state of euphoria, I suddenly realised that if Christ is in all of those people I love and cherish then, without any shadow of doubt, Christ is in me.

God Takes Me
By The Hand Again

I then entered a new phase in my relationship with God. He no longer was a stranger who held himself aloof as He judged my every action, but a friend who lived within me and encouraged and coaxed me along the highway of life and onwards towards Heaven. Even when I fell, He was at my side, encouraging me to try again and again. He was the same God he had always been; it was just now I had a different way of looking at Him.

My reasons for doing things also changed. As I have already said, I was involved with the workings of the parish, simply because it was in my interest to do so. I would have gone to Mass daily to give God thirty minutes of my day. People would not have seen any difference in me or my approach, but I had changed.

I was now involved to help people and went to Mass to thank God for the gift of His day to me. I would liken the whole experience to that of a glass of water filled to the halfway mark. Some people will see it as half empty while others see it as half full. That was me before and after that Cursillo weekend: still the same Johnny; just coming from a different angle.

My way of looking at many things changed at that time (for the better, I hope my family would say; otherwise it is all a sham).

One area, specifically, that changed significantly is my interpretation of the Word of God. Now, I don't mean that I am taking just the lines that suit me, but the realisation that this book, which includes the Ten Commandments, is the greatest blueprint we have been gifted as a guideline for Christian living. It wasn't put together just for the people of 2,000 years ago, but also for us (and all who are to follow us) on this journey through life.

This particular line from Jeremiah came alive for me: *Before I formed you, I knew you,* confirming that God had intended me to be Johnny McCallion long before I was. So my story *did* begin long before December 15th, 1942. Rose Kelly was the means and Mammy and Daddy were the destination, and I arrived. After this, I found myself more open to the promptings of the Spirit of God and, therefore, I was also more open to His people. Not long after this, I started to keep a spiritual diary of thoughts I believe came from God, through His people, into my heart.

Shortly after this transformative weekend, Emmet decided to come home from St Patrick's Seminary in Maynooth. He was in his third year of studying for the priesthood and we found this to be a very difficult situation (if he had dropped out of university we could have told him to pick up the pieces and get on with life), but there was no book to tell us how to support him as he searched within himself for God's will in his life.

We prayed a lot for guidance, as it was all we could do. I had heard that the mystic nun and faith healer, Sr Breige McKenna, was coming to Coleraine to speak at Mass there. I hoped she would have something to say that might give us guidance on how best to help him at this time.

Just before this, during a Search weekend in Termonbacca, we had gathered in the oratory, and some personal sharing was taking place in front of the Blessed Sacrament when Emmet walked into the company and started talking as he hadn't done since he'd come home. As he spoke and told his story of his calling to and from Maynooth by the God

Emmet loved so deeply, I became aware of the Blessed Sacrament and the Lord spoke to me in thought as He said, *you were going to Sr Briege to hear what she could tell you, and I was here all the time, waiting, just waiting, for you to come to Me.*

Once again, I was looking far and wide for the answers that were so close I didn't see them. I told a nun who was on the retreat with us that it was as if we had sent a tulip (Emmet) to Maynooth that was opened wide in the sunlight but that, for some reason, had come back closed, as if in darkness. But then I had witnessed the Son's light (the pun is deliberate) open him wide again that night in the presence of the Blessed Sacrament.

By the way, I did go to Coleraine the following week and Sr Briege gave a beautiful talk. It was nothing I hadn't heard before, as I had a tape of her talking and I had read her book, *Miracles Do Happen*. That is, until the very last minute of her talk, when she uttered the words, 'our faith is like a flower: take it out of the sun's light and it will die'. Need I say more?!

The year after I joined Search, I got involved in the running of the Holy Family Youth Support Group along with my very good friend, George McDaid. We both went into it with the ultimate aim of leading our young people to God by giving them practical experiences of Him at work in their lives and through the actions of others. Just think of the Beatitudes and you have, I believe, the constitution of both of these groups. You see, it is not enough to talk to people - young or old - about God: you have to give them real experiences, made only by providing a listening ear or having a cup of tea or a bite to eat together. Just think, if someone had come to tell me of God and I hadn't met my mother and father, brother and sisters or Sally and the wains and all of those people who have helped make me the person I am today. Do you think, for one instant, I would have listened? I don't think so; I would have been so bitter with life. I'm not saying that God can't touch our hearts Himself (because He can and does), but we are not God. My involvement with the youth instilled in me a new understanding of them and compassion for them; but what it gave me most of all was a great love for them.

I, who came to teach, have been taught. I, who came to give, have been outdone by the generosity of our youth. I, who came to share the Kingdom of God with them, have had it revealed to me in all its glory. I have, it is true to say, suffered much pain because of the very nature of this youth ministry to which my God has called me, but I now know it has brought a tenderness out in me (I am not, I hope, sounding as if I am boasting because I certainly don't mean to) which I wouldn't have acknowledged before. I have also had great joy during this time, but a lot of it must remain locked within the treasure chest of my heart because of the confidentiality promised to those with whom I have walked this part of my life.

There were many times, as I listened to the pain of our youth, that I wondered if I would have been able to cope with life if I had been dealt their hand of cards. I don't know if I could have. I believe that my involvement with them is all part of a greater plan whose magnitude and end I cannot fully perceive. I simply pray I am doing as my God would have me do and not as the world would try to make me do.

During all this time, my mother and father were central to our lives. Daddy had suffered a slight stroke in 1988 and this caused us great concern, but he seemed to make a good recovery from it. Rose Kelly was beginning to slip in and out of my thoughts more often now. I used to say, when talking about her, that I only had one thing that I wished to do and that was to tell her that everything had turned out for the best and I didn't need to know the reasons why she had to let me go. Everything was OK, but only because of the families that had clothed me in security and love.

By 1992, Stephen was going steady with Noreen, Emmet with Edna, Edward with Clare and Catherine with Pat. They all seemed to be very happy with life and I am sure (just as we had been when we were their age) planning for the future knowing that no one had ever got it right until they came along. Mary was on her journey through the education system, having just passed her 11-plus, and was transferring from the Holy Family Primary School to Thornhill College. Around this time, Fr Pat McBride came to our parish. He introduced an hour of centring prayer before the Blessed Sacrament every Saturday evening, from 4-5pm.

During one of these holy hours, I had a strange experience while meditating on the phrase 'Jesus is Lord' and looking at what some people would say is only a piece of bread; the Blessed Eucharist. I was thinking how it would seem to be a contradiction that the Son of God should take on the form of a piece of unleavened bread so that he could fulfil His promise to be with us always.

But He is the God of contradictions. Suddenly, in spirit, I found myself standing amongst a crowd, with a woman on my left reaching out trying to touch the hem of His cloak. He asked me why I wasn't touching His cloak as well. I shrugged my shoulders and said, 'I don't have any problems; I am happy with my life as it is'. Then, just like that, I was back in the oratory trying to figure out what the experience had been all about.

I didn't have long to wait for an answer to that one. On the Friday night of the following week, I came home from the parish draw around 9.30pm and found Emmet in the kitchen. I remarked on the fact that he wasn't away out with Edna as he normally was. Catherine asked if I would like a toasted sandwich and I said I would love one. But I don't think I ever ate it because of what happened next. I went in to look at whatever was on the TV and Sally came into the living room followed by Emmet, and when I looked up I knew something was wrong.

Sally broke the ice by saying, 'Emmet has something to tell you, Johnny'.

Edna was pregnant. What? I was struck dumb; not a word could I speak. I knew I should have been saying something, but what? Maybe I would say something that was said when I was like this child - the innocent child in the womb.

Again, Rose Kelly was coming into my life. For the first time, I sensed the pain she felt and the hurt she may have felt when she had to tell somebody she was pregnant with me. I felt a total connection with her. Oh, how I wished I could undo the situation Emmet and Edna had found themselves in and help return all of their innocence and freedom, which was now gone. I don't think I felt this helpless even at the time of his accident. If only I could take me and mine away from this world and make all things new... but I couldn't.

After a while, Emmet left us to go to Edna and I still hadn't spoken. Sally said she felt that all he wanted from me was a hug and reassurance; that all was well and that we should help sort out the situation for them, as usual. If only we could. I explained to Sally why I couldn't speak or do anything at the time. Catherine came to us and suggested that we should go to them. Edna had a flat in Rock Mills, in student accommodation there, so off we set. We didn't know the number, and as we went from floor to floor in search of them I was overcome with dread that any grandchild of ours would be reared in this dingy place; the baby deserved better. We finally found them up in Magee and the tears flowed freely. Oh, how the tears flowed over the next few weeks (for them; not because of them). It was at this time I realised that we were starting to take on a wider base as a family, because that weekend Clare, Noreen and Pat just seemed to melt into our pain and maybe even absorb it for us a bit.

I went to our family home in Creggan to tell Mammy and Daddy the news. I was dreading their hurt because their grandchildren were their pride and joy. I should have known better; they were fantastic. Mammy said she had thought this crowd were never going to make her a great-granny and Daddy said, 'sure didn't it happen to a bishop' - and it had. There were no judgements, condemnations or recriminations; instead, what came from them was what they had always offered: open and loving arms and hearts. At this stage, Edna was six months pregnant so we hadn't gotten a lot of time to get used to the idea of becoming grandparents - and I was still dealing with the pain within. On the Saturday morning, Sally asked me to go and speak to a priest about the situation, but I knew where I had to go.

I went to the oratory in the Holy Family church that afternoon. Fr Pat lowered the lights and played very gentle background music. After he had exposed the Blessed Sacrament, placing Him on the altar there, I again found myself back in the scenario of the week before. The woman was there and so was Jesus. I didn't at any time see his face or hear him speak, but I sensed it all within my heart - a contradiction, I know, but then isn't He? Remember the piece of unleavened bread.

Now, Johnny, he said, *touch the hem of my cloak and know this: I can heal not just the haemorrhages of the body but also those of the soul, the mind and the heart. I can make all things new again.*

The healing process had started, and I knew that, in God's time, all would be well again. He also told me all that had happened in my life up until then had been preparing me for this moment in time. I wonder? I made Edna and Emmet a promise that every Eucharist I received would be offered up for them until all was sorted out. Emmet had moved into the flat with Edna to support her at this time. I knew how much God meant to him, but just like the rest of us, he has feet of clay. I prayed hard that I was leading them the right way towards You, gently and surely. The days and weeks that followed were not easy for any of us; we all had our baggage to carry and found it difficult to lay it down at the feet of Jesus.

Sally, Mary and I went on holiday to Scotland in early August, and one day, as we were walking hand in hand and talking about all that was taking place within our family, I started to laugh. Of course, Sally wanted to know what I found so funny. I said if I told her the thought that had just hit me she would think I had finally flipped my lid, but she insisted that I explain what it was.

So I told her that I had suddenly thought of Moses leading the

Israelites to the Promised Land through the desert for forty years, and how, at the last moment, he was taken away from them and so he didn't see them reach their destination, but reach it they did, because the Lord was with them and guiding them.

'What has that got to do with us?' asked Sally.

So I explained that we, as parents, aren't unlike Moses: we lead our children through this desert of life (hopefully towards God and heaven) for around forty years, and because of the rule of order, in most cases we will die before them, leaving them to make the final part of their journey in the presence and guidance of God, just as the Israelites had to. And guess what? They made it to the Promised Land and so will ours. So let us once again put our trust in God. Only he can see what the future holds. He never promised us a rose garden; only that He would be with us, even to the end of time. Our pain is His pain. Our joy is His joy.

In the early hours of Friday, September 25th, 1992, our granddaughter Marie was born and our pain was eased. A child had come into our midst and, with her, love blossomed. I can remember going over to see her that morning and the fear I had within me. I can remember touching her cheek with the back of my little finger and the shake in my hand as I did so. I can remember, too, the tears that came to my eyes and the lifting of the heavy load that had been mine since June. The child had come as God's gift for all of our pain. For a long time, I feared getting too close to her as I knew Marie was not ours to keep but only to share in. I had to battle my way through that one, but battle I did, and am I glad that I did. A new generation was now on the move. She was perfect.

I wondered if Rose Kelly ever thought of me and the journey I was on. Here she was creeping in again. What would she think of Sally and the wains, or did she even care? Did any of them bear any resemblance to her in looks or mannerisms? I could only wonder. Around this time, I believe God was preparing me for all that was to come. *How?* I hear you all say. By bringing me closer and closer to Him, day by day.

My love of and need for the Holy Eucharist was taking on new dimensions and so I would go as often to Mass as I could because it was then that I felt so close to Him, and it was then that I could tell Him about all of my needs (and sometimes my wants) as I knew He listened intently. I can remember one night, when I was out working with the youth of Search, something happened that made me very angry. I just felt I was being used and abused by a certain situation; so much so that when I got home I said to Sally that I was 'no more than a taxi driver'. The next day during Mass, as the priest held up the Eucharist, I asked the Lord to come and change my heart and take away the feelings I had within me, and show me what he wanted of me. Within one hour, I gave a lift to a lady who was late for work and running to get the bus. She had made herself late by doing something for her mother and so had asked God to send her a lift. She said to me, 'do you know what you are, Johnny? You are God's taxi driver'. Need I say more? He has never failed to amaze me.

During all of this time, I was deeply involved in the Search group and in our own parish youth group. Through both of these groups, I have come to know God in a very special way. He is a God of love, compassion, understanding and hope. He is also the God of pain, brokenness and woundedness. And he is the God of total resurrection. That is why, when people ask me how can I be bothered with young people, I now just laugh; how could I explain all of this to them? I am sure they don't have the time it would take for me to explain to them that it is only as a result of a lot of giving and receiving that I feel the way I do about the youth today.

I also found myself reaching out for all the spiritual aids that I could muster - and there are many as we struggle to come closer to God. The one thing I have discovered is that we must have an openness about us to let Him in, as He will never force Himself upon us. That's the main difference between Jesus and people: He will always respect our right to privacy. One of the greatest aids (apart from the Eucharist) is the sacrament of reconciliation. I used to fear going to a priest to confess my sins despite being reassured so often throughout my life that everything said was in the deepest confidence. That all changed when my God showed me how He stands, with tears continually flowing down his cheeks, and then, in Spirit, He went on to explain that I was the one who decided if they were tears of joy or of sorrow.

How can that be? I remember asking.

He replied to me in thought: *When you sin you turn away from Me, causing My tears to be those of sorrow. When you seek reconciliation and turn back to Me, they become tears of joy. The priest is only the channel through whom God's graces flow.*

At Mass one night, I was asking God to send more young people to the youth group as the numbers had gone down to six the previous week. When the Gospel was read, it was about the healing of the ten lepers. Later on, at Communion time, Jesus said to me in thought: *Johnny, remember that even though only one returned to give thanks, I still cared for the other nine. So don't worry about those who don't come, but be there for those who do.*

He was saying, *numbers don't matter: just do My work and trust in Him to do the rest.*

Many times, as we work with young people, we are called on to share in their pain, and one of the hardest things to explain is disparity when it comes to material possessions. How can I talk to young people of a God who loves them all equally when their home situations can be so varied? With this thought in mind one day, as I stood in an oratory filled with young people, I asked Him to explain equality in God to me.

He said: *The young and not-so-young people all have within them My Spirit. So, tell them this: you are all a temple of my Holy Spirit; none more or less than the other. Even when you turn away from Me, I am waiting for your return.*

This is the God who I have come to know and love. Every so often He asks me to go on a journey I would not choose of my own free will, but when it is complete I then can see where He has been leading me.

Around this time, I (and later Sally) got involved in an annual peace pilgrimage walk, from Derry to Knock, for inner peace, followed by peace in our hearts, homes and our country. Central to all of this is the deep devotion many people have to Our Lady, and so their belief is that a Son will do as His Mother asks. So our prayers and petitions are offered to Jesus through Mary. I remember one day, while praying the Rosary, stopping to ponder the question, *how can I pray through someone that I don't really know?* So I asked Jesus to make me more aware of how Mary fitted into my life, and he said in thought, who do you think has hold of your other hand?

He was referring, of course, to the vision I had of him leading me through life as He held my right hand in His and he was telling me that it was Mary holding my left. I thought of the nun who had led me by the hand that day in the corridor of Nazareth House when Mammy and Daddy stumbled across me, and then I thought of all the times in my life that Mammy had taken my hand in hers.

It was simple: Mary was working through them. From that day on, my relationship with and understanding of Our Lady deepened.

One day, as I was contemplating the fifth glorious mystery of the Rosary - 'The Crowning of Our Lady Queen of Heaven' - I tried to imagine the crown Jesus would have placed on her head, and the jewels or whatever would have been used to adorn this crown. I thought about this for a long time, and I became aware - just a wee bit - of the great love He had for His Mother.

I thought, *sure wouldn't it make the love that I have for my mother fade into insignificance, and believe me I would use all of the precious earthly gems for Mammy's crown.*

I realised, then, that it would have to be a very special crown for Mary. Then the thought that struck me was that Mary's crown had been adorned with the souls of those who had come to the Father through Mary, and how it is being added to, daily, by those still coming to God's Kingdom through Mary. So I pray continually that me and mine will one day be added to that crown.

One thing that used to bother me greatly was if I was to die and be honoured or privileged enough to go to Heaven, how could I rejoice if one of mine on earth was still grieving my going? This constantly troubled me over many years until, one day, I had the following thought: *You will be in Heaven because then you will know all that lies in store for those who come after you, and time in heaven is non-existent. This lesson He taught me at a later date.*

What about choices in this life? As I have said, Jesus will not force Himself on you. You must invite Him in, but once you do, you have decisions to make. I remember asking Him what He wanted from me, and He told me He wanted nothing but for me to listen to the following and then decide what I wanted for myself: *You are all like a grain of sand: you can either end up as part of the hard road or choose to become like a piece of glass - crystal clear and a beauty to behold in the eye of God.*

These are just a few examples of the many times my God has brought me closer and closer to him, especially over the past few years. It is all part of His ongoing preparation of me for today and whatever it holds. Finally, to those who would ask me why I would spend my time ministering to youth, I share this simple verse of joy that filled my heart so much that I wrote it down:

He has given me a jewel beyond compare,
Shown me a world without despair,
Given me a way to walk with Him,
And leaves me a hope that stays within.

That is why I will always be open to the call of our young people - because they helped open me to the call of my God.

Letting Go Of Those We Love

Life was changing for me and mine. Sally and I had to face up to the fact that the boys and Catherine were moving on and making lives of their own. The emptiness of our home was unbelievable. Firstly, Emmet moved out; then Stephen and Noreen bought a house and he moved out. Catherine, who had been home from university because of illness, had returned to Belfast and Edward, who had graduated, had taken up a placement in America.

So, in the autumn of '93, within six weeks our home had gone from being full to just Sally, Mary and me. I suppose Sally and I were so wrapped up in what we saw as our loss that we missed the obvious:

Mary also was suffering. It was her brothers and sister who had gone. Just a word of caution to parents: don't just assume that young people don't care or that they can cope with strange situations better than we can - they have the same emotional needs we have.

That Christmas was a very mixed bag indeed, particularly for Sally. Her brother Stephen, who had been working abroad, was knocked down near his home a few days before Christmas and was seriously ill as a result of the accident.

So, with Edward not being home and Stephen ill in hospital, I think we just about spluttered through that time.

Stephen made a very slow recovery. He often questioned why he had survived when people who had been hurt as seriously as he had often didn't make it. But, as I have said many times, we can't explain God's ways.

Around this time, the young folk started to make plans for their weddings. First to go were Stephen and Noreen, then Edward and Clare. This period should have been a very joyous time for our family, but over the happiness hovered the spectre of death. You see, on the day our Stephen married Noreen, Sally's brother Stephen entered hospital for what should have been a routine test on his throat.

The following day, while being prepared for the test, he went into shock and then into a deep coma from which he never recovered. He died on October 16th, 1994. Who can explain God's ways?

For us, the process of letting go was not over yet. In many ways, it was just the beginning, for the next year was to see us being asked to let go of both Emmet and Catherine as they made their plans to marry. Emmet and Edna got married in June and Catherine and Pat in August.

Both occasions were a time of great joy and festivity (just as Stephen's and Edward's had been in spite of the sadness we felt about Sally's brother) and a time of welcoming others into our family.

These were also times when Rose Kelly come into my mind, and I wondered again (not for the first time, may I add) if she would be proud of me and mine. I knew that Mammy and Daddy were.

We were also blessed with two gifts during all of this time. Caoimhe and Matthew were born to Stephen and Noreen, only eleven months apart (the same as our Edward and Stephen). They have come to claim their own space within our hearts. *So much more for me to tell Rose about,* I thought (there she was creeping in again).

In early January of '96, Emmet got a job in England; an answer to many prayers. Then, shortly afterwards, Daddy took his second stroke in eight years - but this one was worse than the last.

Was God going to ask us to let go of him as well? Edna and little Marie left in early March to join Emmet in Calstock, Cornwall, to set up home there.

And so, again, we were asked to let go. *How much more Lord... how much more?* This question kept repeating itself over and over to me as I came to the conclusion that I didn't want to let go of anyone or anything, but accepted that let go I must.

In March of '96, I took part in a week of guided prayer. I needed something to refocus my faith in God because I felt I had been letting the world move in on my life and letting God move out of it somewhat. This week was hopefully a way of refocusing my faith journey.

In guided prayer, you are invited to sit with a piece of scripture and focus on the characters - and indeed on the storyline - of the piece and you are also invited to become a part of the scenario or situation (if you wish to do so).

One piece, in particular, resonated with me: the story of Bartimaeus in Mark 10: 46-52, which tells the story of a blind beggar who, because of his faith, has his sight restored by Jesus. Immersed in those words of scripture, I became that blind man: I couldn't see, but I could sense the presence of the Lord and crowd and the heightening of the excitement and anticipation as He came nearer to me. So I called out to Jesus as he passed by, even though I couldn't see Him.

Jesus stopped and called me to Him and asked me: *What do you want me to do for you, Johnny?*

I replied, *Master, that I might see again.*

I wasn't quite sure what triggered the sequence of events that were to unfold over the following few months, but something had. Had God's time come? Whatever it was, the quest to tell Rose Kelly that all was OK suddenly began to gather momentum. Where and when would I start? What would I do if I found her? How would I cope with Mammy and Daddy? And, if I did find her, would I like what I found? Would she want to know me? What if I found out that my conception was a deep source of pain to her?

These questions, and many more, ran around my mind for what seemed to be an eternity. *You will hurt your parents if you go looking for her.* That thought, in itself, was one very big obstacle to my undertaking this journey. It felt like it would be a total betrayal of their love - so freely given to me over the years without conditions. And then, after so much agonising, the penny dropped and I realised I was using them to cover up my greatest fear: rejection (again) by Rose Kelly.

But fear could no longer be the deciding factor because I now knew I didn't have a choice: if anything were to happen to either of them, I couldn't go looking for her, as I would be betraying their memory. So it had to be now. *But how?* That was the question. I knew my name, her name and my date of birth, but that was all; nothing else.

Fifty-three years had elapsed since I was born. I didn't realise how much stress I had been under until, one day, I took a tingling in my fingers that was so bad I phoned and got an immediate appointment to see my doctor.

A lot of people (myself not least among them) have reason to be thankful for his devotion to his patients: I am talking, of course, about the late Dr Tom McGinley.

He didn't hand out pills willy-nilly, but rather listened to and then talked to his patients as a friend, giving them sound advice. In my case, he told me he thought my problem was stress-related.

I realised that he was right - and also what it was that was causing me such anxiety. I took a few days off work to see if it would help, but it didn't. I had to face facts; Rose Kelly was the source of all my stress.

I had no choice... I had to go and find her.

PART TWO

THE LONG DARK TUNNEL

Removing The Mask

Author's note:

The next several chapters of the book focus on a period in 1996 that turned out to be the most traumatic time of my life. I kept a diary at this time and I believe the best way to convey the profound emotional turmoil I was experiencing then is to publish those entries for you to read.

They start with an entry from April 23rd, 1996, and end with one from October 8th of the same year.

The excerpts reproduced here aren't meant to hurt anyone. My hope is that they can act as a guide to help anyone who may be on a similar journey to mine (or thinking about embarking on one).

And so, for that reason only, what you read will (bar some editing for the purposes of clarity) be faithful to the words as they were written.

* * * * *

Tuesday, April 23rd

I am so confused, Lord; so agitated. I feel as if I am being pulled apart; this way, that way. So many demands. I hope it isn't sounding selfish, but where do I fit in? I give, I give and I give. Part of me has given so much.

I now realise I was prepared to wear the mask to cover it all up. Time to take the mask off. Time to go seek out my past roots. For so long, I said I couldn't as it would hurt Mammy and Daddy if I did. I now know it is only the fear of ultimate rejection that holds me back. I must take the chance; I must take the risk.

* * * * *

Wednesday, April 24th

Today, I have decided to phone and start the process of searching, firstly for my birth certificate, then to register with the adoption registry in Belfast. What do I do after this? I don't know. I will wait and see what unfolds.

* * * * *

Friday, April 26th

Search weekend. I am so tired; I really don't need this. We also have a feis on Sunday to raise funds for our parish youth group. Lord, give me the strength and energy that I need to do your work.

* * * * *

Wednesday, May 1st

The mood swings I am experiencing at this time are nothing ordinary - this isn't like me at all. Lord, how I need to feel your presence around me! The young people are something else, Lord.

They, apart from Sally, Mary and the others, give me a reason to go on, to keep my eyes firmly fixed on you, Lord.

* * * * *

Friday, May 3rd

Youth weekend. The young people work so hard, Lord. I am aware of your presence here among us, Lord, and in each other. I thank you, Lord, for your peace.

* * * * *

Tuesday, May 7th

Today, Lord, the tiredness has returned and so has the confusion. I feel so drained and the pull towards something I have no control over is now immense. People think I am tired for the wrong reasons. They don't know what is going on in my mind. Questions such as, 'What if I *do* get information that brings me into contact with my natural mother, and she is maybe already dead or doesn't want to know me, and if she does, what do I do then?' dominate my thoughts. So many possibilities, yet no easy answers. How I love the people in my life, now, at this moment; they'll never know how much.

* * * * *

Wednesday, May 8th

I have, after a lot of prayer, made a decision to leave Search. The reasons are mine, and mine alone. Just to say, I am happy with the decision.

Friday, May 10th

This journey has to be mine, and mine alone; that is one of the conclusions I have come to. I have to love everyone enough to protect them. But Lord, why so much darkness, turmoil and confusion?

I seem to be surrounded by a great mist that doesn't seem to be clearing. I suppose I expected some sort of reply by now about my birth certificate.

Saturday, May 11th

Today it arrived; an address. No 88, Botanic Avenue, Belfast. My gut tells me this isn't the one that matters. It's unlikely anyone living at this address now would have any connection to Rose so I doubt I would find many answers there. Where do I go now... or do I go anywhere? Only time will tell.

Monday, May 13th

This has to be about more than a piece of paper; she is not just a name on a register. I wish the despair I feel at this time would clear. It's as if I am on a course that I can't get off, but the scary thing is, I don't know where it is going.

Tuesday, May 14th

Today I called at home to see Mammy and Daddy. As I left them, I made up my mind to forget all about it and to leave well enough alone. I have worn the mask this length of time; I can wear it a while longer. We shall meet in the next world and she will understand when I explain.

Ten minutes after making that decision, I met a woman who asked me to pray for her sister's mother, who was ill. She explained that she (the sister) was adopted, and ten years ago had decided she must find her natural mother - not because she didn't love her mother and father, but because something inside of her needed answers.

She then told the story, finishing up with the fact that the lady in question was now dying and that her sister was glad she had sought her natural mother.

I couldn't speak (she didn't know my story); then she caught on that something was wrong with me. So the search goes on. I put my hand in the hand of the man who calmed the waters again. Don't ever let go of my hand, Lord.

* * * * *

Thursday, May 16th

I have now identified the source of the agitation. It's coming from God, and I know from experience it's only when He wants to show me something that is for my own good that He does this: takes me on a journey I wouldn't choose of my own free will.

Why does He let us go into the wilderness? I have been there before and I have come to realise that it is always before we come into the oasis.

So maybe He is sharpening our senses for this great time. What seems to be the dark night of the soul may be this time out of the Son's light. Oh, how I pray that mine all come to know You as I do, and come to realise it's not all about material things, but rather spiritual well-being and awareness of God in their lives.

I feel I am being pulled through a time tunnel into an era I don't know. I have a great fear of the unknown. I feel as if I am running downhill and gathering speed, with no brakes to slow me down or to stop. I wonder why this quest has become so urgent. It is as if someone, or something, is pulling me along. It seems as if there is a definite time schedule that I must keep to at all costs.

* * * * *

Monday, May 20th

I have pondered. I have wondered. I have questioned as I have never questioned before. I have lived many possible scenarios - all to no avail because unless I go down this road I can't find the last pieces of the jigsaw. When will I go? I don't know. But I now know... my sanity is at risk if I don't.

* * * * *

Tuesday, May 21st

We must get in touch with the child who is deep down inside each of us; only then can we face ourselves and grow.

* * * * *

Wednesday, May 22nd

I am going back to work today. I must get on with everyday living. I must get order back into my life. On my way to work, I realise that I must do something positive to tell Rose Kelly that all is well, so I must go back to the source; to the beginning. I must go back to the Nazareth House in Bishop Street. I must go to those who know.

Sr Bernadine, the principal of the school, welcomes me with open arms and promises to help me get as much information as possible. Sister expressed surprise that I should have been in the Nazareth House in Bishop Street at all, as it was an all-girls home.

This backs Mammy's (fairy) story that I was just passing through and that she and Daddy had gone looking for a little girl and met me coming along a corridor with a Sr Teresa. How chance changed all of our lives... but was it chance?

* * * * *

Friday, May 24th

Sr Bernadine rang and confirmed no record of me in Bishop Street or Termonbacca. How I sense the blind man reaching out towards the passing figure of Jesus. How I sense Him ask me, *what do you want, Johnny?*

Even though I was only around one year old or thereabouts. How I feel my hand in His as He takes me to them, introducing us and telling us to be one as in family (I am the blind man, I need so much). Oh, such great love my God has for me. Such great love I have for you, Mammy and Daddy. Sister has asked Nazareth House in Fahan to carry out a check. She will let me know as soon as possible.

Into The Unknown

Monday, May 27th

What a surprise! Sr Bernadine rang at 9.05am with news; my birth mother came from the Draperstown area. I went from Belfast to the Nazareth House in Fahan on February 15th, 1943, when I was two months old (what I was doing in the one in Bishop Street that day Mammy and Daddy stumbled upon me is a question that will have to remain unanswered for now).

Now the hunt is real. I don't know how I feel. I suppose I didn't expect answers as quickly as this. Now the reality: I have a place to go, I have a starting point. I have also realised I may have a very big decision to make when I get all these pieces of the jigsaw together. I may have to turn away again if my presence causes too much pain or disruption in her life... if I find her.

It's not Draperstown itself, by the looks of it. I have seen Fr Frank O'Hagan, a priest I know who is based that area (in Straw, just a mile outside Draperstown) who has kindly agreed to help me with my search. We have checked the records. But it may be nearby Desertmartin, which isn't on the computer yet. He will check and let me know as soon as possible. I had checked out a few addresses for Kellys in the Draperstown area that I had taken from my work computer. I travel about that area a lot in the course of my work so it's easy enough done.

I told Fr Frank I didn't feel any sense of Rose Kelly's presence as he questioned (or rather, gently coaxed) me to reveal my reasons for and feelings about this search at this moment. I told him I didn't know why I was on this journey at this moment in time as I was always very happy (and still am) with the people to whom God has led me and who care for and love me. That I have not come looking for a mother, father, brother, sister, family or friends as I have all of these people back home in Derry. For some reason, I feel this journey is about releasing someone (I don't know who, be it Rose Kelly or whoever) from some kind of bond.

We discussed many things that day, and among them was the question of who, if anyone, did she name me after? As I said, I had checked the computer at work for any Kellys in Draperstown that might ring a bell; in particular, I was looking for a Rose Kelly (just in case she hadn't married) but she wasn't there. Nothing was there to make me feel I was closing in on anything. It was then that I thought of my own names - John Joseph - and typed that into the computer. Lo and behold, there was a JJ Kelly listed, with an address in Iniscarn Road, Desertmartin. Might be a relation, I don't know.

On my way home via the Five Mile Straight, I thought to myself, *you have given up too easily,* so I decided to head back towards Desertmartin and try to find this Iniscarn Road and check it out. The first place I stopped at was the church of Christ the King; at least, I think that's what it was called. It was surrounded by a small graveyard. I made my way through it - again shooting in the dark - and found a grave that held John Kelly and Teresa Kelly (died late 1940s), but no particular feelings did I get while I was there.

I then decided to find the address and drive past the house; I never intended to knock on any door to cause hurt or disruption. This was one of the many things Fr Frank and I had talked about and it was one of my requests: until we had all of the facts put together and had come to a decision on what was to be done, no one - but no one - was to know of me. I didn't find the road and eventually gave up, thinking, *you have had enough for today; leave it until later.* Anyone who knows the roads in and around Desertmartin will know that, to get there from Glenshane, you would enter the town from the Tobermore Road; but to go to Derry from there you would leave by the Desertmartin to Draperstown road. This I did, and I was driving along when, suddenly, on a very bad bend, a sign caught my eye at the bottom of a small road to my left: *Iniscarn Road.*

I turned back and proceeded along this narrow, twisting and turning road, keeping an eye out for anything or anyone that would trigger something within me. As I made my way upwards, I passed an old church (again, with a graveyard surrounding it) and I thought, *I must check it out on the way back.* I reached, and then passed, the house, but didn't find anything or anyone that looked familiar. Back down the road to the graveyard I drove.

I entered by what was the main gate and proceeded to meander my way along and down through the graves on my left-hand side. There were a few Kelly graves but nothing that gave me any feelings of being mine, so I took myself and my thoughts along the bottom part of the graveyard. I remember thinking to myself, *you really have looped the loop this time. What do you expect to find here? These people can't answer your questions.* I had turned to go up the other side when I saw them: two marble headstones amongst what was a collection of grey, granite-type headstones.

The first I approached had a John Kelly, who died in 1968, and his wife Kathleen, who died in 1985. Could this be my natural grandfather and grandmother? In the other grave was a Rose Kelly, and my heart missed a beat until I read the date of her death: May 7th, 1927. Could this be my birth mother Rose's grandmother? Both headstones carried the townland name of those interred there: Brackaghlislea. For some reason, I feel I have stumbled onto something. Another one of my gut feelings; only time will tell.

As I left Fr Frank that day, we discussed our tactics: he was going to see his parish priest and I was going in search of baptismal lines and any other records that may be filed away and we would meet up again whenever. No date, no time, no place. And so to Derry and Sally I did go, and to all that she and it holds for me: security and love.

A Time For Reflecting

Tuesday, May 28th

I have been asking myself, in the middle of all of this, *is it only for you, Johnny, that you are doing this?* I don't think so. It's for Edward, Stephen, Emmet, Catherine and Mary, and for all those I must let go of so that they might live. It's for Sally, in particular, because she has lived this nightmare of mine. She has been there when the memories (yearnings, really) or callings took hold of me, supporting me through it all.

Someday, maybe, I will share this journey with you, my family. Maybe you will read it for yourselves; whatever, you are very much part of my reason for searching. We must all know our origins. To the grandchildren who are here (Marie, Caoimhe and Matthew) and those who are to come, I owe it to you so that you will also have a history; a complete picture.

To those of you who can turn to me and put a title on our relationship - be it son, husband, father, granda, brother, sister, friend or confidant - I must have a beginning and an end on this earth; otherwise the picture is incomplete.

I also need to thank Rose for the gift of life she gave to me and to all of you, because if she hadn't done so, all of our lives would have been different and I... well, I wouldn't have been writing this entry in this diary. I love her for that. The miracle she started continues tonight, for I feel the baby within Clare's womb is moving. It's for you, kid! God bless you.

I have often wondered what she is like and if any of us resemble her in any way. Do we reflect her nature? Do we, without knowing it, fulfil her hopes and dreams for all of us? Then again, does she ever wonder about me and mine? Does she, like I do, pray that God protects us all until the time is right for us to meet (in this life or in the next), or are her memories of my coming into her life (I don't know the circumstances surrounding my conception) too painful for her to even want to remember? Most of all, I would just love to say, 'it's all right; reasons don't matter'. All is as it should be, because if she hadn't let me go I may not have been in your lives the way I am, and that's why it's all right - without all of you, I am nothing.

Since I met Sr Bernadine, a peace has come over me which convinces me that this quest is God's will because only He can give such peace. The walls are falling so fast it is scary.

* * * * *

Thursday, May 30th

I have come through such pain these past few months. The biggest cause of this pain has been guilt at the feeling of betraying Mammy and Daddy. This has been the biggest obstacle. How I have prayed to God that the opportunity would arise so I could make it right before anything happens to them. I love them so much. I am doing this search now before anything does happen to them because I know I couldn't betray their memory after they are gone. I have so much to tell her about them.

Often, I think of how they didn't have to take on the responsibility of us; they could have had a carefree life, and that makes me feel so humble and special. I surely have been blessed by all of the people God has brought into my life. I have gone on guilt trips over the past; especially now with all of the horror stories that are unfolding in connection with orphanages.

Why did I escape? I have cried for those abused children and I have prayed for them, and I have asked myself, *why wasn't it me, Lord?* As I say, the walls are falling so fast now. I am approaching the time of decision.

The new life is here. Conor is with us now; God bless him and them! Clare and Edward are so happy (as is Sally and everyone) and so am I. Again, my emotions are mixed. I can't help wondering if there was any of this joy and celebration when I was born. What were her feelings on that day, December 15th, and what are her feelings now? As I wonder, I wish my emotions could be free.

Pieces Of Paper

Friday, May 31st

I am after my baptismal lines; maybe something there will help answer the unasked questions.

Phoned some churches in Belfast; finally got some help from a priest at St Ann's Oratory who referred me to St Teresa's and I left a message with the lady who answered the phone regarding my quest.

She said Fr Fullerton was out but that she would get him to give me a ring. He did this, but by then I was out. He said I could ring him in the morning.

* * * * *

Saturday, June 1st

Rang Fr Fullerton. He said there was nothing on his records but suggested two other churches - St Brigid's and St Malachy's - which might be possibilities. I left the details with a very helpful lady at St Brigid's and then she asked for my address in case she found anything.

My next call was to St Malachy's, where I spoke to a priest who had been chaplain to the Nazareth House. We talked a lot in a short space of time and he checked his records.

Nothing there, but he suggested that an outside possibility was the Church of the Holy Cross and he wished me well. So, next to the Church of the Holy Cross.

The lady I spoke to (a nun, maybe) seemed to be into counselling and talked to me about different areas. She promised to do all she could for me.

I then decided to live in the real world for a while and go out and cut the grass. While toiling away at this, Fr Fullerton rang back; something was bugging him. 'Johnny,' he asked, 'where did you get married? Because they would have had to send those details to the church where you were baptised to update the records. Good luck again.'

Sometimes we are blind to what is under our noses, so back to St Mary's in Creggan I did go, but they were in the middle of their First Holy Communion Masses and certainly didn't need me intruding. I will call later on Monday or Tuesday.

The day moves on; the agitation is growing. I can't wait. I must know today. So, around 3.30pm, I rang St Mary's and Fr Brady answered.

I explained my mission and, because Mammy and Daddy are on his sick list, I stressed the need for confidentiality. Not that I ever thought he would break it, but that is me at the moment - stroking every 't' and dotting every 'i', just in case.

Father starts to tell me there is a procedure that must be followed in cases like these.

One must go to Bishop Street (Catholic Family Society) and have a social worker appointed to do the investigating on one's behalf and to be guided by them. I told him that I was so far down the road that neither he nor the social workers could catch up with me, and either he got me the information now or I would get it elsewhere.

He then said, 'hold on a minute', and I said, 'next week will do', and again he said, 'give me a minute', so I did. And then he gave me the information I so badly wanted: St Brigid's, Derryvogie Avenue, Belfast, December 19th, is the place and date of my baptism.

No one knows how it feels.

Joy of joy, another piece of the jigsaw has fallen into place! I rang St Brigid's to tell them; they had already posted the certificate. Someone somewhere is the guiding hand. *But who and why?* That is the question.

* * * * *

Tuesday, June 4th

Agitation is moving me again. I have decided to have a search done to see if I can turn up some birth details regarding my natural mother. Mrs Eva White, the lady who works in the General Register Office in Belfast, said that this could take some time.

I decided to cover the years from 1895-1930 because I can't just assume she was a young girl when she had me; she could also have been an older woman, who knows?

Sr Bernadine is checking Nazareth House in Belfast for details of my whereabouts prior to going to Fahan.

* * * * *

Wednesday, June 5th

Today I called with Fr Frank.

He said he had a few leads in his part of the search and asked in more detail about my own family.

A very curious question was, did we have any twins in our family?

I just wonder what he is looking for. In a strange way, I feel that he suspects she is dead.

He talked about a lady on his home visit list who may know something about my birth mother.

He also said he felt that a brother or sister would know more about her than nephews and nieces. So, is she dead?

That is the question I must ask, and what are my feelings if she is?

Today we celebrate another addition to our family. Edna has given birth to a son; Kevin is his name.

We are separated from them because of Emmet's work situation, which is very difficult for all of us.

We would just love to be able to be with them at this joyful but difficult time.

* * * * *

Thursday, June 6th

I can't explain what happened today, or even what prompted it, but I put together the words and chords of a song and was able to sing and play it (on the guitar) by the end of the day.

It goes as follows:

I Went To The Well

I went to the well, my tale there to tell,
One of great doubt, guilt and pain,
There I met me a man who said take my hand,
And your heart I can cleanse once again.

Now the world had moved in, and I'd turned to sin,
I didn't know how I could tell,
Then I looked in his eye and I heard him sigh,
Then I knew all was well deep within.

So I reached out in hope, I had nothing to lose,
But such a great lot I could gain,
Then I felt his first touch reach the depth of my soul,
And I knew I could love once again.

So won't you take the chance, just give him a glance,
And open now wide your heart's door,
Not just you and me but the whole world, you see,
Can learn to love once more.

(Repeat verse one, changing 'cleanse' to 'heal')

Reconciliation would seem to be the strong theme. How did I do this? I don't know. The only explanation I can come up with is that it was another very much God-led and God-filled experience, and I can only think that. Reconciliation is central to all of our beings.

A Mother's Fears

Sunday, June 9th

Today, Mammy and Daddy were down to see us, and after I had left them up home, Sally and I were chatting.

I had, at an earlier time, told her that I thought Mammy suspected something was up, and today Sally related the following story to me: while Sally and Mammy were washing the dishes, Mammy started talking about a woman we all know who has two adopted children, and how the woman was willing to help them look for their natural parents if need be, and how this attitude shocked her.

Sally then asked her how she felt, and Mammy went on to say that, even after all this time, she still fears a knock at the door from someone from the past.

Remember, this is the woman who has been my mother for over fifty years, and still she fears someone from that far back coming to claim me.

People would think that the adopted child can be insecure, but what about the adoptive parents and their fears and doubts? Sally said, 'Johnny, just go up, put your arms around her and give her a big hug and kiss, then tell her you love her'.

If only it were that easy; I have done so on many occasions but obviously it wasn't enough to ease her fears.

I have to do more. I have to confront her fears and lay them to rest. So now, Lord, I pray again for your guidance as you lead my steps onto the right path and protect my words. Please Lord, let my love shine through for her and Daddy - no matter what.

* * * * *

Monday, June 10th

Today, the agitation is so strong, but this time it is all to do with Mammy and Daddy and our very special God-given love. Between working and praying, I wrote the lyrics to another song (the second within four or five days) and composed the music.

This one is called 'God's Plan'. I don't know what's going on at the moment; in fact, it's mind-blowing. I thank God that I can identify His hand in all of this by the very awareness of His presence and input.

The words are self-explanatory and are as follows:

God's Plan

We know that we are special, we know God had a plan,
It's his wish that we're together, long before this time began,
He knew that we would need much love,
and oh such tender care,
And the road we had to travel,
sure he said that you should share.

We are special because of your love,
we are special because you're rare,
It makes us one in God's love and this is what we share,
It's a privilege, it's an honour, a journey beyond compare,

The time will come when we must part,

and what's been done is done,
But a love that's planned in heaven, can overcome this one,
So don't fear those who are in our past,
let's live this love that's ours,
It's in our hearts, we know our own, and here we build our homes.

We are sisters, we are brothers, we are family and clan,
We thank you both for saying 'Yes' in answer to God's plan.

I have no doubt that all of this is God's plan that we are living out; my only problem is trying to continually figure out where is it leading to rather than being still in the presence of my God and letting Him take control at this time of great turmoil and pain. So often I have told others to be still and feel His love and presence in their lives. So often I have proclaimed that He is with us always. So often I have given such advice to others, but sure this is different: it's me who is involved this time. Lord, let me listen to the sound of your voice.

* * * * *

Tuesday, June 11th

Today is 'D-day'. I have struggled with how I should approach Mammy regarding the revelation she made to Sally on Sunday. I have decided to take the bull by the horns - easier said than done. I headed up to Creggan and was in the house for over an hour, talking about everything and nothing, if you know what I mean, before the opportunity presented itself for me to proceed.

She said she must go out to the kitchen - the same kitchen in which I first told her that I knew I was adopted all those years ago and where I told her that it didn't matter, for as far as I was concerned she was my

Mammy and I loved her and Daddy and no one else. Now, over forty years later, I am on the same mission to reassure her of my love for both of them. Didn't I make it clear enough over the years or has she forgotten?

We got out there and I asked her to give me a hug and then I held her in my arms (as I have never held her before) and gave her a kiss. Then I said I had something that I wanted to say to her and that I wanted her to stop, for once, and listen.

She said, before I could get any further, that she wasn't dying, referring to my hug and kiss.

So I told her not to try to distract me, and that a long time ago I had said something which she obviously hadn't heard clearly - either in the first instance or else with the passing years she had forgotten. I said I was surprised to hear of her conversation with Sally on Sunday regarding her fears that someone from the past would come knocking at their door.

'Mammy,' I said, 'I told you then and I tell you now: there is no one from the past, present or future who can come between us. You and Daddy are the only parents I have ever wanted.'

Then she laughed and, poking me on the shoulder, said, 'and I am telling you that there was no one else before us in your life'.

To which I said: 'Let's stop it there. You don't have the right to say that; I am the only one who can. So, please... don't ever have any doubts about my love for you.'

She then kissed me and said, 'I must make your father's tea'. That's my Mammy: always giving and always (in her own way) avoiding reality.

* * * * *

Wednesday, June 9th

Called in at home today, just to check that all was OK. You would have thought that yesterday had never happened: everything is back in its allotted place. And that's OK as well.

* * * * *

Friday, June 14th

Still no answer from the register office regarding Rose Kelly. Maybe tomorrow. Isn't that the story of my life? *Maybe tomorrow.* But will tomorrow ever come?

A Call From The Grave

Saturday, June 15th

Still nothing; maybe Monday.

* * * * *

Sunday, June 16th

Oh, how the mood swings are coming and going. Here I am in the midst of my own; we are all gathered in our back garden and the craic is ninety, but part of me is so detached from everyone. Part of me must press on and I am so agitated. I just hope no one else senses how I am at this moment; I don't want to put a cloud over anything. At times, I wonder if they can even touch in on my feelings because part of this is part of them; so, somehow, they must.

* * * * *

Monday, June 17th

I phoned the General Register Office this morning as nothing, still, has arrived in the post. I spoke to Eva White and she explained that this type of search is more prolonged and could take a while yet. Then we started chatting about the progress of my search; she asked me when I had first found out that I was adopted, thinking I had been seeking my history since then. She sympathised with me until I explained that I had really only started, in earnest, on May 22nd of this year. She expressed surprise at how much information I had acquired in such a short space of time and finished by saying that someone must be looking out for me or over me. I said I had no doubt who it was and then we talked of God. She is a lovely lady.

She said she might have information later that day and I said I would ring her tomorrow morning. Once again, the agitation is driving me: there is something about the grave in Desertmartin that is bugging me and it seems to be central to whatever is going on just now. I must go back. I went back (I am not long home). I entered the churchyard by the same gate, deciding to retrace my footsteps of that first day (that first day seems so long ago now; so much has happened since then - or so it seems). I went down one side, along the bottom and turned to come up the other side of the church. *My God, how did I miss it?* How was it that I had tunnel vision when I first found this grave? I hadn't even noticed the fact that someone else was in this grave: Francis, who died on April 7th, 1966. The inscription read:

KELLY
Francis, died 7th April, 1966
and his wife Rose, died 7th May, 1927

This Rose was a young woman at the time of her death. So it wasn't Rose's grandmother (as I had thought on my first visit) but could, in fact, be her mother. *The couple in this grave is Rose's mother and father,* my gut was telling me. Still confused, I drove away and decided to journey up the Brackaghlislea Road, which I had noticed on my way to the grave earlier. Up I went, up and up through the crossroads and on up, but I didn't see anyone or anything that would raise my curiosity. I did wonder if this was the road she would have walked as a young, carefree girl and if this was the area of my origin, but all of this was conjecture - I had nothing concrete to go on. I couldn't even go to Fr O'Hagan with my latest discovery as I had nothing to back it up.

So back down the road I went. I was driving on the main road home to Derry when the car phone rang. It was that great lady, Sr Bernadine, with another bit of information; another piece of the jigsaw. The Catholic Family Society in Belfast now had possession of the Nazareth House records; she gave me the telephone number. Car phone still in hand, I rang straight away and spoke to a Sr Noeleen. I explained exactly what I was after and the progress I had made to date. She asked me if I had a social worker helping me with this; I told her I didn't but explained Fr Frank's role in all of it.

She then said, 'you are so close - you don't know how close'.

I asked was there an address for Rose Kelly and she said there was, but that she couldn't give it to me over the phone. I then asked was this a Belfast address and she said she couldn't say, whereupon I said it mustn't be because my search was concentrating on a townland in the Draperstown/Desertmartin area. She remarked again that I was so close and said I needed a social worker on the case. It turns out even Sr Noeleen didn't know just how close I was.

At that precise moment, I was less than 200 yards from Brackaghlislea, which I am now fairly certain is the townland where Rose Kelly was from. It lies between Draperstown and Desertmartin. Sister made a few suggestions regarding who I could contact and I asked her if Fr Frank could gain this information if he phoned her. She said she could only confirm information if he were to provide it. All the time we were talking, I had been writing everything down on a white paper bag, so me and the bag were off to Fr Frank; after all, I was less than ten minutes away from Straw parochial house.

I arrived, and as I passed his office window I looked in and there he was, sitting at his computer with his back to me. As I rattled the window he turned his head to look, turned away and then turned it back quickly when he saw who it was; he said he had been sitting thinking about me. Then he asked me what had brought me to Draperstown today, as we hadn't made any arrangements to meet. I explained about the urge to go back to the grave, and then he said, 'come on in'. We talked about all that had happened and I told him of Belfast and the information being held there.

He then said, 'Johnny, tell me: what is drawing you to this grave?'

I explained how I felt it was central to my search and to my belief that buried in that grave were the mother and father of my birth mother, Rose Bridget Kelly. He said I never failed to amaze him and that he would phone Sr Noeleen in Belfast and see what information was on file. This he did, explaining his mission and confirming an address for the Rose Kelly who had given birth to me.

Then he asked her the following question: 'Does this, in any way, tie in with another incident, sometime in 1940, when a Patrick Kelly was born?'

My heart nearly stopped. *Something isn't right here,* I thought; *this has nothing to do with me. Who is Patrick Kelly?*

He then whispered, 'I'll explain shortly what's going on'.

Now the fun began. At this stage, I had been standing up and Fr Frank said: 'Why don't you sit down? I have something to tell you, and while I need one more piece of information to confirm that your Rose Kelly and the Rose Kelly who I have been tracing are one and the same, the coincidences are too many. Firstly: the grave you are being drawn to is that of my Rose Kelly's mother and father. Secondly: on my sick list is a lady who was very close to Rose, and thirdly: your birth mother's address is given as Brackaghlislea on your file, and my Rose Kelly also comes from Brackaghlislea.'

Fr Frank, on whatever pretext, had visited this lady who was a friend of Rose's, and during this visit started to talk to her about Rose and her whereabouts. She had left the area as a young girl and gone into service in Belfast. Did she ever have a child? Yes, came the reply. Was it a boy or a girl? A boy, who was born and baptised in Belfast. Fr Frank said he thought he was home and dry when he asked, 'was this in 1942?' and she said, 'that would be about right'.

So his next question was, did Rose Kelly ever bring him home? 'She did', said the friend. 'He was reared at the family home. Patsy is his name.'

Father was thrown by this last piece of information and said his first thought was that maybe it was twin boys that had been born to her: one was kept and raised while the other (me) was given up for adoption (it was only later, when he checked parish records for a 'Patrick Kelly', that a likely match came up with a birth date of 1940 and he realised Patsy had been born to Rose before she'd had me).

He asked her did Rose have any more children. No, she answered. What happened to Rose then? The friend explained Rose returned to Belfast and they lost contact with her for over ten years. Then, around 1960, she met and married a merchant seaman called Ted Cappelman and went to Filey, West Yorkshire, to live with him. Father then gave me a list of names from the parish records of Rose's brothers and sisters, again touching in on the coincidences. The first, born in 1912, was a set of twins: Mary Alice and John Joseph; it was he that Fr Frank thought I was called for. He went on to give me other names but I said I didn't want them until I knew for certain that this was the right Rose Kelly, who, incidentally, was also a twin.

'Father,' I said, 'there is something you are not telling me... when did she die?'

I asked him that because I was now sure she was dead. I knew I had put this man on the spot. He was trying to soften the blow, as he saw it, by explaining that it didn't end there and this was a very big connection and that it really was only the beginning and, given time, I would probably get to know them all.

'Father, tell me when she died,' I asked again.

'She died in 1984,' he said. It was as he'd said; this wasn't the end, but the beginning. And yet... Rose is dead, so that door is firmly closed to me. She had no family by Ted, who had, he said, died three years after her.

'How do you feel?' Father asked. And ask he may; I was angered by the revelation that she'd had another child - born before me, by the sounds of it. I couldn't refer to him, as Father did, as my 'brother'. He was reared at her family home in Brackagh... so why did I have to go?

Numbness, confusion, blankness (and I don't know what else) describes how I feel. I pray she found happiness when she married. She was 42 years old. Oh, my dear Jesus, what is going on? How has this turned out this way? I fear if I reveal my existence, what will it do to her reputation? But if I don't, what does it do to me? I don't know how I feel.

Overwhelmed by panic and turmoil, I realise I must get home to Sally, security and all that is mine. No one knows how much of an eternity that journey home seemed to take. I stopped along the road and phoned Sally to say that I was on my way and that I would fill her in on all that had unfolded today. I remember thinking, as I drove, *what happened to Rose Kelly? What did the world do to her, dear Lord... what?*

By the way, I also found out today that I appeared on the records of St Joseph's babies' home in Belfast on January 25th, 1943. It is yet another piece of the jigsaw; and what a jigsaw this is turning out to be.

When I arrived home earlier this evening, for some reason I had the white paper bag on which I had written down all of the earlier information plus whatever data I was capable of writing that Fr Frank had given me. Standing in the kitchen of my own house, I held it towards Sally and she said, 'Johnny, you and your bits of paper' as she put her arms around me and just held me in her arms. They were arms of total security and love. Oh, how I love this girl of mine. Oh, how I need her; now more than ever.

Confusion Reigns

Tuesday, June 18th

I didn't do much sleeping last night. I tossed and turned all night long, eventually getting up around 6am. What the hell is going on, Lord? I feel so confused. Someone I have been seeking is dead, and though it would seem she never told anyone of me, my gut feeling is telling me differently. Eva White has confirmed Rose's date of birth as July 9th, 1918. That's one day out from Fr Frank's date, but then Sally pointed out that twins have been born either side of midnight before and have, because of this, different birth dates. Again, Eva remarks how even this search fell into place, telling me that a letter was about to go out in the post with this information and that also asked if I now wanted a copy of her birth certificate.

Of course I did. Aren't these pieces of paper very important to me in all of this? So she is organising this for me. Another shot in the dark has hit the mark - or has God once more revealed His involvement in all of this as He cuts through the obstacles and speeds me along this road of questions and answers? I know what I think. I feel so confused, bewildered and belittled. Who can tell me about her and who can tell them (her family) about me? As I said before, Rose had a twin sister - christened Mary but answers to the name of May; does she know? Where am I going to go to now, Lord, where?

Numbness surrounds me. I have been aware of our Mary very much over the past while and how protective she is of me, but I feel that I must explain to her my reasons for going on this journey of discovery. She loves her nanny and granda so much and isn't that beautiful? So do I. I say to her that I am not looking to replace them or to even put anyone on a par with them because they are my mother and father; they and they alone. We spoke for a while about all of this and I told her how much she and the others mean to me and how their love has carried me at this time. She is now aware of all that has been revealed. I hope I made it all clear to her. I love them all so much.

* * * * *

Wednesday, June 19th

Another restless night; another mind-troubled day lies ahead. Why bother with it all? Sally asks me how I am feeling. 'Who are you talking to? Mr Nobody?' I reply. That's how I feel. I see the pain on her face but she can't feel the pain in my heart no matter how close she comes to me. They say you always hurt the one you love; Sally, if I did, I didn't mean to. I am hitting out at the world. Back to Mr Nobody: that's who I am, origins unknown, no one can tell of me, no one knows and does anyone really care? These are some of the thoughts running through my mind as I looked at photos of the wains (the future) while thinking of the past (Rose Kelly). Why was he (Patsy) kept at home and why did I have to go? I know all of the logical answers but I just can't accept them right now. Oh, what pain. No one knows the feelings I am going through. I still can't help feeling that someone knows about me, because if I am her birth son (and I am), then part of me is part of her and I can't believe she could have kept quiet about it for that long; that, for 42 years, she didn't mention me to anyone. Do you believe it? I just wonder who she told; that's the question.

I have made an appointment to see the social worker in Derry for next Thursday. Maybe there is something on file in Belfast; I have to know. I took a photograph of myself at Fr Frank's request and included photos of the wains. I don't know whose face may trigger it off. I also included a letter to whoever might read it explaining my reasons for coming into their lives at this time. I really am shattered. I haven't even started to deal with any of the things that have come out of these past few days. I have put them on hold and into the appropriate pigeonholes until the time is right. How I need Sally. How I need God. How I need everyone.

Johnny Let Go

A new personality - 'Poor Me' - has made his appearance on the scene today to accompany Mr Nobody on his way, and why not? Haven't I had a raw deal? Everyone but me has had it their way: Patsy grew up knowing the land of his mother, and maybe even his father, Rose got her freedom and Mammy and Daddy got their child.

But poor me. What did I get? I really know better these are gut reactions. 'Johnny Joe' is what they called me; those who wanted to acknowledge my birth, that is. 'Johnny Let Go', they should have called me. I know it's not me, or is it? I am so hurt and so angry, I don't think even I know how I feel.

Maybe this will help touch in on my feelings. Did you ever see a beautiful Easter egg sitting in a shop window, in a lovely box with colourful paper wrapping it up and all held together by the biggest ribbon you ever did see, and think to yourself, I must buy that one, did you?

Then you take it home, dying to open it up on Easter Sunday morning.

Finally, the great day arrives and you open it up only to find, to your horror, that your beautiful egg is not what it seemed to be. Why? Because it is shattered and broken in many little pieces inside. That's me. Can't someone put me together?

I went to see the social worker. She was a very nice lady but didn't have any real answers, because the reference to me in this file, which was so hard to get at, consisted of just two lines and nothing more.

One thing she mentioned interested me, though: another file relating to the time before I was adopted, when social workers would have been working toward the finalisation of my adoption by Mammy and Daddy, may exist. This may or may not contain information regarding me that may throw some light on the matter.

Only a few people can get access to these files, and only if they have approval from the courts. I'll put this one on hold for a while. I can also do what is called a trace of the children of Rose Kelly, though, at this time, this too can wait. I have so much to do before that.

After school time, I met Sally and took her to the grave. She just can't figure out how I found it in the first place. I can, and I know who guided me there. It was today that I left the letter to go with the photographs in case Father makes contact with one of Rose's friends; you see, I am in control again - or so I think.

Tonight, I cried tears, tears and more tears. No Mr Nobody, no broken Easter egg, just me; that's who needs to know. Cry and grow (the child within).

The social worker said she felt we should be approaching 'your brother' (as she termed him) to find out what he knows. But I only have one brother: Kevin. He is my brother. He and no one else; no one. And that's the way I feel about it.

* * * * *

Friday, June 21st

I awoke this morning with tears rolling down my cheeks; how they flowed. I looked at Sally and she asked me what was wrong. I said, 'please don't ever leave me', and immediately realised that this wasn't fair to her. I so much fear being alone in the crowd again. My emotions are in total disarray (again). I don't even know where I will go from here. I haven't even thought about what comes next and people are telling me that I must be allowed to grieve. For who or what, I ask? I didn't know Rose Kelly so how can I even begin? I must get to know her before I grieve and let go of her. Here we go again, Johnny Let Go before it has even started. But I have nothing tangible of her so how can I even do that?

Everything feels so confused and unreal; this isn't happening to me, or is it? I seem to be looking in on something, but I don't know what. Thank God for God, He keeps me sane. If any of you (the wains) read this and have lost your faith, just go to the well and the Man there will take away all of your hurts if you tell him I sent you (I am only joking, Lord). Lord, I feel so much guilt. I feel I am betraying someone very special to me; not Mammy and Daddy this time, but Kevin - I don't think he can even suspect how I feel about him.

* * * * *

Saturday, June 22nd

I am trying to step back a bit and live in the real world and see it for what it is. I have so many blessings. First and foremost of these are you lot; if you read this you will know who I mean. Then Mammy and Daddy, Nuala, Kevin, and Marian. Do I need any more? But guess what? I do have a lot more; my God has been good to me.

* * * * *

Sunday, June 23rd

Today my friends from Cursillo went to Belfast to take part in a practice walk for the annual peace pilgrimage from Derry to Knock, joining with the Belfast pilgrims, who will be walking from Armagh to Knock at the same time. I must be honest and say that it seemed an ideal opportunity for me to do a bit of tracing of my history while I was in Belfast. The group were starting out at 10.30am so I said I would join up with them at 1pm. I also wanted to thank Fr Fullerton (the priest at St Teresa's in Belfast) personally for all of the help he has given to me with such an open heart. So off I set into the unknown, in search again of things from the past.

Firstly, I went to see Father, who was only ten minutes away. I met him as he stepped out of his car. I really don't think he realises how much of a help he has been to me. Then he directed me to St Brigid's (the church in which I had been baptised), but I missed it (or, at least, I didn't see it) and somehow found myself in the university area of Belfast, driving parallel to Botanic Avenue. This was the address that was on my birth certificate; number 88, to be precise. I don't know what I expected to find there, if anything. After all, it was over fifty years ago and a lot has happened and changed since then. Anyway, I parked in a side street just opposite it. I came out and stood on the pavement on the other side of the street and I couldn't believe my eyes, because I didn't know if someone was trying to deliver a message or if they were trying to take a hand at me. Why? Simple really: the sign above the shop window I was looking directly at read, *Bag and Baggage*.

Someone... but who and why? That's the question. I walked across the road onto the footpath. What was I thinking as I walked? That this is the first place that I had come to that I knew for certain she had been. Along that street she must have walked; it really did feel strange. I lingered for a while and then lingered some more; then I knew I had to move on. I asked a man if he could direct me to St Brigid's church and he asked was it the new one or the old one and I said, 'whichever one was in use during the forties', so he said it was the old one and duly gave me directions. I was there within minutes. It was sited behind the new church, and when I pulled up outside I couldn't believe my eyes. It was completely boarded up and all of the windows were blocked. I just stood there in total shock. Am I never to find what I am looking for?

While I was standing there, looking at another dead end (or so I thought), a priest passed by and asked what was wrong. I explained and he insisted that I go to see the Monsignor. This I did, and I was glad that I did. We chatted about the whole situation and I thanked him for his and the lady's help when I was looking for my baptismal lines. Then he said, 'maybe you would like to see the actual entry'. At last; something tangible. The only part of the entry that I was in a position to confirm was, in fact, wrong: it said under the 'marriage' entry that I had married Sarah Teresa Quinn - not Quigley, as it should have read. He changed it then and there after I had explained that I had phoned and spoken to him earlier. I am glad to reclaim she who is definitely my wife.

Sally, I love you so much. Because of you, I can carry on with this journey and take of risk of being hurt because I have your arms to hold me and your shoulder to cry on.

Onwards I Must Go

Monday, June 24th

I am so tired, but somehow the journey must go on. Part of me wants to stop now, but something else is pulling me along this road. It has happened again: just when I had justified in my own mind why I should pack it all in, I meet another person who starts talking about something which, to them, would seem completely unconnected to me, but that, to me, is filled with significance. On this occasion, the person told me of their involvement with the children at the primary school in the Nazareth House. This woman talked about how her own life experience alerted her to a need in boys which wasn't necessarily as deep in girls. She was referring specifically to children who were in the orphanage of old - not to the schoolchildren of the present day - and the fact that so many didn't know of their origins. She felt that boys were more insecure about it and that it led to problems in later life.

I then said that she had turned an earlier decision of mine on its head and explained the situation. She said, 'Johnny, go the whole way'. For some reason, I still think that the person who Fr Frank has made contact with holds the key to it all. I just wonder.

I took myself to Gulladuff today. It's a village about eight miles past Draperstown, just on the other side of Maghera, where Patsy now lives. I got his address off Fr Frank. My decision to go there was triggered by something Father said to me earlier on in my journey when I told him about the time I drove through Draperstown and three different people had waved to me as if they knew me. I had wondered who they thought they were waving to. He had said jokingly: 'Why don't you take yourself over to Gulladuff and see how many people call you Patsy; then we will know if there is any resemblance.'

I called with the local priest, Fr O'Donnell, in the hope that maybe he would identify something in me that would ring a bell, but he didn't. In fact, he suggested that I call at the local bar and see if the barman made any comment. I told Fr O'Donnell that I didn't even wish to meet him (Patsy) yet and that I didn't know if I ever would.

I just don't know how I feel. I left it at that and asked that if he could add anything which might be confidential, he contact Fr Frank O'Hagan, whom he had already spoken to regarding this matter.

* * * * *

Tuesday, June 25th

Today, I decided to get a copy of Rose's marriage and death certificates and also to start a trace for any other children she may have had. To do this, I phoned Eva White in Belfast. It's nearly as if she is my own personal researcher. I told her all that I knew. Married 1960. Where? Maybe Belfast. Died 1984, most likely in Filey. She said that it really wasn't a problem, but if I could get some more information it would help. I said I would go back to Fr Frank. I did, but he wasn't at home; he was out doing his sick rounds. I wonder if he will find anyone who can tell him anything about me. I left a message for him with Marie (his housekeeper, who was another great support at this time) and said I would ring later.

Around half four, Sally rang to say Fr Frank wanted me to call him right away; there was something he had to see me about. I hadn't told

Sally about the latest phase of my search yet. Fr Frank answered the phone and asked if Sally had told me about Ted Cappelman? I said she hadn't - what about him?

'He's alive,' came the reply from Father. 'I have an address for him - or I will have within 24 hours'.

Someone is trying to get rid of me, was the thought that struck me there and then. *The Kellys would rather have me over in England as coming to them and bringing shame on them.* Father went on to say there was more but that he wouldn't talk on the phone. I arranged to call this Thursday at 1pm. Wednesday night is the England v West Germany match and I am sure Fr Frank would want to see it. Sally asked what Father had said and I told her. She then asked if that was all, and when I told her it was, I knew by the look on her face that there was something else. So she told me that Father had told her there was something I might not want to hear. Now my mind was looping the loop again. Really, is there anything they could tell me that I hadn't already mulled over in my head many times in preparation for this? Do they for one moment think it makes any difference to my mission?

Here are a few of the thoughts that are with me just now: had she turned to drink and/or prostitution? Was I conceived as a result of rape or abuse (both are really the same)? Are there more children like me? Maybe she had never wanted me, maybe she didn't know my father (the result of a one-off encounter) and maybe they will try, in some way, to blame her death on me.

Then again, maybe I am overreacting; I don't know. But the egg is shattered again. I am sorry I didn't set up the meeting for tomorrow. Maybe if I didn't give a damn for other people's feelings it would be easier to deal with all of this, but I do, so it isn't.

I then shared a thought with Sally as we talked about the latest revelation (that Ted Cappelman was, in fact, still alive) that had been given to me by some 'kind' person (or people) in Draperstown.

'They are treating me like the long lost bastard, Sally,' I said. I can still see her face and hear her voice as she said, 'don't call yourself that. Don't ever call yourself that again'.

'But it's what I am, Sally, it's what I am,' I replied. 'I can't change it, no matter what the world says. I am part of her and they can't take that away from me. They may try - and I am only supposing, here - to drive me away from Draperstown, but this time I will make the decision when the time is right for me to go: me, and me only.'

I don't think anyone really knows how I feel; not even Sally. She can sympathise, but this pain isn't hers; it's mine. How I need her and the wains more than ever. By the way, if one or all of the scenarios that I outlined regarding Rose Kelly are true, it doesn't make the slightest bit of difference to my opinion of her. She is still the lady who gave me the gift of life and I love her for that.

This whole business can be funny at times and then it can be devastating. I never personally had any difficulty regarding what some people would term my 'illegitimacy'; I never had any identity crisis. I am who I am - Johnny McCallion - but the revelations of this journey can only be dealt with because of my secure background and loving home.

I wonder about all the others who haven't been as lucky as me and who have set out on this journey hoping to exchange their present situation for a better one. They go on a journey of hope only to be splattered and tangled. To whom do they run? Dear Lord, wrap your loving arms around them; they need to know you. As I said, I am sorry I didn't arrange to meet Fr Frank tomorrow. But I suppose I've waited 53 years, so what's another day?

* * * * *

Wednesday, June 26th

What's another day? I'll tell you - this is how I feel today: in total panic, turmoil and I don't know what. I wish it was tomorrow, with all of its fears revealed, so I can just get on with it.

* * * * *

Thursday, June 27th

Today I may face my greatest fears, but I always knew the risks when I embarked on this journey. Enough to say that I will make any decisions of importance, in relation to my life, that need to be made. Because this is *my* time, and I have come in peace. I ask God again never to let go of my hand. I think I have covered in my mind every possible scenario that can unfold. So... here goes.

* * * * *

Author's note:

I wrote the above entry in my diary on the Thursday morning just before I was to go and meet Fr Frank and made no further recordings in my diary for the next two days.

I was so caught up in events that I didn't have the time or emotional headspace to put pen to paper.

For that reason, the chapter that follows is not from my diary but is my own recollection of what unfolded over those two momentous days...

Today With All Its Fears

Thursday had finally arrived. I was running a bit late for my appointment with Fr Frank so I rang him (just in case he may have thought I was backing out). I explained I would be about fifteen minutes late; he said that was OK. The journey there is really a bit of a blur to me, as I spent it going over and over in my mind all of the possibilities.

I had decided to bring my diary with me and I didn't really know why except that I felt I had written my fears into it and I could show them to Father if they came out. It is very easy for us to say 'I knew this' or 'I suspected that' when someone tells us something we had pondered in advance of today.

When I arrived, I parked the car and walked to his front door. On the way there I had to pass the window of his office and had got into the habit of looking in first to see if he was there. If he was, I would rattle the window.

Today was no different except for one thing: when I looked in, a lady was sitting in his office. She had seen me so I couldn't turn back. I would have if I could.

My mind was spinning; my thoughts were in disarray. I didn't want to meet anyone at this time. *Why has Fr Frank done this to me?* I thought. *Why?*

If only I could get away; but there was no way back. Fr Frank came to the door, asked me to go to the sitting room and said that he would join me as soon as possible.

He apologised for the delay and the fact that Marie wasn't around to make a cup of tea. In my head, I called her all the yellow so and soes for having got offside, as I saw it. But I should have known better; she was away buying custard powder so that she could sweeten us up later on (only joking, Marie).

Time on your own at a time like this can make you conjure up some strange thoughts and call people some not very nice names, and, believe me, that was what I did. I could hear the mumbling of this person in the other room, and of course I was putting two and two together and getting a hundred.

This 'man of peace' was anything but at this moment in time. Eventually, I could make out her voice, Father saying, 'I'll see you later' and calling her by her name. I suspected who it was but I was barking up the wrong tree; this lady had nothing to do with my mission. He then joined me in the sitting room, apologising for the delay and asked me how I was. I think I said, 'alright', but I don't really remember; Father knew I was on edge over what was about to be revealed.

He asked me what I thought of the news that Ted Cappelman was alive. I replied: 'They are trying to get rid of me and keep me far away from here, but I will decide when and if I go or not, because the last time I went, I didn't have very much of a say in the matter, but this time it will be a lot different.'

Then Fr Frank said that some other things had come to light, and I suppose when I think of it, the following part could not have been easy for him to relate. Firstly: Rose had not died in 1984, as we'd been informed, but in 1980.

How could they get it so wrong? *Something isn't right here,* was my thought. The date of her death was given as January 6th, 1980. Fr Frank then gave me Ted's address in England. So that's what it's all about. *Big deal,* I thought. *Is this what I have gone through turmoil for over these few days?*

But it wasn't; there was more. At the time of Rose's death, Father said, Patsy and his cousin, accompanied by their aunt Alice (Rose's sister), were the only ones to go to the funeral. Alice, by all accounts, was a great support to Rose in the bad old times and a lady who I am really sorry I never met (nor will I ever meet; she died in 1986).

On the way there, she told them that they would meet two young people over in England and that they were not to tell anyone in Draperstown of them. You see, when Rose married Ted, she took to England her two children whom she had reared in Belfast on her own: a girl called Kathleen and a boy called John.

As Fr Frank spoke, my mind was reeling. *Oh, Jesus what's happening? What has gone so wrong?*

All I wanted to do was tell her, 'it's OK'. But it wasn't OK, and the tortured thoughts continued. *Why are these obstacles being thrown in my way? She didn't even leave me my name; she used it again. Mr Nobody: that's who I am. Patsy, she left in Draperstown; Kathleen and John she kept with her; but what did she do with me? Let God carry me!*

I don't even know if God came into it for her. I felt so hurt, devastated and angry. I wanted to hit out. I wanted away from that place; as far as I could get. I wanted back to Derry. I needed to get there as quickly as I could, otherwise I didn't know what would happen or what I would do. Father asked me if I was OK. I can't remember what I said (someday I must ask him).

He then went on to say that, being the man he is, he decided he should check this out before he told me. To do that, he could only go to one person: Patsy. Patsy knew about himself, so Father knew he could speak openly to him about me without fear of telling him something of himself that he didn't already know. So he went to Patsy, explaining he had a friend who had undertaken a search into his background and the paperwork had revealed that Rose was his natural mother.

Father asked Patsy if he knew anything of this. He said he didn't. They must have talked about the journey to England and the rest, and then Father said to him that for someone who supposedly hadn't heard anything of me, he found his reaction strange. Patsy then told him the following story:

He said he hadn't reacted to this revelation of my existence simply because this wasn't the first time this sort of claim had been made in relation to Rose by someone tracing their past. Roughly ten years before, a fellow from Coleraine had come: he had been born in the 1950s and been put into foster care when he was six months old, then later adopted by a Protestant couple and reared as their son. Jimmy Stratton was his name.

Numbness and confusion (plus a host of other feelings I couldn't even describe) raged in me. *This can't be happening,* I thought. *It just can't. This isn't what I came for.*

Father was using terms like 'your brothers and sister', but my brother and sisters were Kevin, Nuala and Marian - no one else. *No one.*

We talked about all of it and I put it all into emotional pigeonholes (marked, 'to be dealt with later'). I am sure I asked questions, but what they were I can't remember. He stood up; I can remember he had something in his hand. He said he was going out to organise a cup of tea and that he would leave me on my own with my thoughts, and also with a photo of someone who he felt that I was ready to meet: Rose Kelly.

He went, and I sat with the photo in my hand for several moments. It was face down, just as he had handed it to me. I had traced the story and now it was time to face the storymaker. It was time for my past to become more than pieces of paper, time for it to take on an identity; a real person. I began turning the photo over... it felt so unreal. Why?

I'll tell you why: it was unreal because my Mammy and Daddy were in Derry and this lady, who I couldn't call mother, seemed so remote from it all. Again, my thoughts overwhelmed me. *The pain I feel is immense. I am torn to shreds, as David with the lions - I hope he didn't feel this pain. This will all take time.*

Father returned and I put on the mask again. It was something I had become very good at, having had plenty of practice over that past while, in particular.

Only the love and security that I had at home were keeping me sane. That, and my belief that, 'God knows me, just He as knew Jerimiah, long before he formed us in the womb'. You see, I am a child of God - that's who I am.

The tag the world would attach to me doesn't in any way change that. I am Johnny McCallion.

I remember saying to Father that I had to get home and there I would gather myself. *Maybe I will continue; maybe I won't,* I thought. One of my biggest anxieties was this: *If I reveal myself, what do I do to Rose Kelly's reputation?* I wondered what this world had done to Rose Kelly that drove her away from her homestead. Why did she seem to reach out for love in (what seemed to me) the wrong way and in the wrong places?

'I have worked with youth,' I said to Father Frank, 'and have so often seen them confuse sex for love.'

Is this what had happened to her? I wondered about that a lot.

Finally, I left Father and Marie (I had opened my story up to Marie on the very first day I had sat down with Father in the parochial house. Her mother and my Daddy were full cousins. As I'd said to Fr Frank at the time, 'she will wonder what is going on and I trust her enough not to break my confidence'). And so, to home.

I had phoned to say I was on my way. Sally (oh, my Sally) was waiting; all I could say, sarcastically, was, 'I'm going to hire the Guildhall and hold a family reunion and wait to see who turns up'. I told her all that had been revealed. I couldn't tell how she felt about it all simply because, at that time, I wasn't capable of feeling any kind of emotion myself.

It's time to gather forces, I thought. *Time to withdraw from the battlefield and take stock.*

The Water Of Truth

I haven't written anything since Thursday. Why? Because it all seems so unreal. I don't even know if I have truly taken in any of what Fr Frank has told me. Maybe I will wake up and all will be as it was.

Deep down, I know it's all real. Deep down, somewhere beyond any place I have ever gone, is the source of it all; the well to which I have to go, to drink the water of truth, to meet the man who wants to heal all of my hurts and take away this awful numbness.

I suppose the nearest I can come to explain my feelings is that I am like Joseph, whose coat of many colours was stolen by his brothers. After everything that has happened in the last few days, I, too, feel as if something is lost to me.

Nothing that has been revealed over the past weeks will ever change my opinion of Rose Kelly, the lady that the world would probably have stoned if they knew her story (and most likely did). I thank her from the bottom of my heart for this life of mine and for all of us who, in some way, are in her debt.

Pain, I have much of, confusion is in abundance... but so is love. So I will hang on to love. It is another step in getting to know Rose Kelly (I call her this in love and affection; I would love the world to call her 'lady'). I must do that before I can ever decide to let go. How I love my

Mammy and Daddy! They are God's gift to me. Thank you, Lord. They give me strength - even though they don't know it.

* * * * *

Sunday, June 30th

Today I told Edward, Stephen, Emmet and Catherine; I just told them on the phone. I am so fragile, I was afraid of breaking down in front of them. It was the only way I could do it.

Who Is My Brother?

As I have said, I decided to put everything on hold - or so I thought. I was driving along up our road on my way to get the daily paper when the following conversation took place in my head:

You can't just leave it there.

What do you mean, I can't? Why can't I?

Because you have stirred up something in the fella in Gulladuff.

The fella in Gulladuff... Patsy.

I have no doubt who was prompting me: My God. His Spirit was saying differently to my will, but that has happened before to me and He was always right in the past. I came back to the house and got Patsy's address, though not with the conscious intention of doing much with it that day. And then off to work I proceeded; one has to live in the real world now and again. I had appointments that day in Garvagh.

Normally I would have gone directly from Dungiven, but, for some reason, I headed over the mountain to Maghera - another impulse. I don't quite know how, but I ended up at Gulladuff, at Patsy's front door. I knocked. No one answered so I went away and I don't know if I will be back again; that's me at the moment.

I arrived back in the office around noon and decided to see if there was a phone number for Jimmy Stratton, the fella who had gone to Patsy ten years before claiming to be Rose's son.

The operator said there was only one number listed for a Jim Stratton in Coleraine, so I took it down. Worth a shot. I rang the number and a young lad, who I assumed to be his son, answered and said his father was at work. He's a postman and would be in around half one or two, he said. I told him who I was and said I would ring back around two or half two. I had to say that, otherwise I may not have made the call.

I rang as arranged, but I didn't know what to say; one doesn't make this sort of call too often in one's lifetime, I suppose. I introduced myself, saying this was an awkward situation for the both of us, and asked him if he wished to meet. He did. *So it's him, alright,* I thought. *I need to get this over and done with as quickly as possible.* We arranged to meet at the bottom of his street at 6pm that evening and go for a cup of tea somewhere - neutral ground, at my suggestion. He was waiting at his own front door and waved to me to come up the street.

As I drove up, I knew who he was as he was so like Rose Kelly. He asked me to come into his home. This I did - despite how awkward I felt. His younger son was in the sitting room, and Jimmy joked about how a photo of his daughter was really his son dressed up; same kind of humour as me. We started to relax a bit and talked about the many things we had in common. Central to it all was the drive to know the past and all its secrets. Jimmy was amazed at how much information I had gathered in such a short time; I explained I had planned the whole thing with the help of my God, and that's how I felt.

His wife, Edith, joined us after about half an hour and soon she was taking a full part in our conversation. At times, I could sense her pain for the both of us as we talked of the things that had come to us over the years; the yearnings and all things we had wondered about.

I have always, I suppose, had a very positive attitude about how special I am, so I very much shared this as I talked of the things I had found and the answers I felt I had gotten. I reinforced the point of my main mission and talked of how Rose gave us the most important gift of all (and maybe it was the only thing she could give us): life. It was up to us what we did with it.

Jimmy shared with me the story of his search. He had known Rose had fostered him out at six months of age, finally giving him up for adoption when he was around three years old.

To me, the saddest part was that, as she handed him over to the foster mother, she also gave her the last two and sixpence in her pocket so he could be cared for (the Lesson of the Widow's Mite has nothing on this one).

He talked of how, having searched around Fivemiletown in Tyrone because of wrong information given to him (by his mother, though not deliberately), his journey finally took him to the Draperstown area. There, he met Patsy, who had taken him in around the family homes as a friend. My blood ran cold at this (and I said so to Jimmy) but he said that they were very nice people and he had a cup of tea in one of the homes. Big deal. Big, big, deal!

I then said: 'If I ever go into their homes it will be as Johnny McCallion: eldest child of Eddie and Mary McCallion and born of Rose Kelly. Not as a 'friend' of anyone - they have denied me for too long to get away with that one.'

I shared with Jimmy and Edith the words of 'God's Plan' and 'I Went to the Well', plus another piece I am working on. Hopefully, they will mean something to him. He asked me if I had met Patsy and I said I hadn't. I told him of this morning's journey and the fact that I didn't know if I would ever go to him. I then asked that he keep my visit secret in the meantime, explaining that this was me at the moment.

The meeting, which I thought would last half an hour, went on, in fact, for four hours, and as I drove home I thanked God for His presence and promptings; because of Him, I had met a very special person in Jimmy. He is, indeed, Rose Kelly's spitting image.

* * * * *

Tuesday, July 2nd

The phone rang in the car around 10am and the voice said, 'I can't contain myself, Johnny, what happened yesterday evening?'

It was my old friend Sr Bernadine. I met her yesterday and told her of my proposed meeting with Jimmy. I laughed and said, 'I will see you in fifteen minutes, so don't go out'.

We talked about everything that had happened and of all that I still had to do: find out exactly where Rose is buried, visit the grave and then, when the time is right, have a Mass of Thanksgiving for Rose Kelly. Without any hesitation, Sister offered me the use of the Nazareth House for that.

I said: 'There is one thing that would make it complete, and that would be if Mammy and Daddy would be there, but I know that would be impossible'.

She reminded me of the God who had moved mountains for me and said He could sort it out; I know that He can.

Then Sister said, 'Johnny, you know that there is something else you must do'.

I knew what was coming.

'You must write your story - if not for yourself, then for others, so that you may help people going through the same pain that you are experiencing now.'

I replied: 'Indeed I do, Sister, It is for that reason I have been keeping a daily diary of my journey and putting my feelings and experiences into it, so that when the time is right for me to deal with all that has been revealed, I will be able to unlock the pigeonholes one by one and deal with them at my pace and in my way.'

We talked of how it didn't have a surprise ending, but how certain strengths had carried me through. I had always said that someday, I would. I had even decided on a title for the book: *Never Let Go of My Hand.* I have decided to write this book - though, if it's ever published is another question. I stood up to leave this great lady when she reached around me to the wall behind me and said, 'there is something I want you to have as a memento of our journey together', and she took down a plaque of Isaiah that bore the inscription, *I have carved you on the palms of my hands.*

She said: 'This is very special to me, Johnny, and maybe, someday, I will tell you why.'

I replied: 'You don't have to, Sister... I saw it all in your eyes.'

* * * * *

Wednesday, July 3rd - Friday, July 5th

Over these past few days I have started the book. It has taken me a long time to come to this point. I have realised that if I am to have any chance of coming to terms with the fallout from all this, then I have to start at the very beginning. I am putting together the framework and then I will add the meat. When will I finish it? I don't know. Only God can answer that one.

* * * * *

Saturday, July 6th

There is much rejoicing today; Conor was christened. There was also sorrow because Emmet, Catherine, Edna, Pat, Marie and Kevin aren't here. But that is Sally's and my pain and it can't be allowed to take away from Edward's and Clare's joy. We must keep all within our hearts; but then, Sally and I are experts at that by now. It is so nice to be among my own, and this special day went on well into the night. I also managed (don't ask me how) to do a bit at the book. You see, I was surrounded by the people who have made me who I am.

* * * * *

Monday, July 8th

Today, while I was calling with a customer in Garvagh, the agitation returned. So I asked the customer to check the phone book for a P Kelly, Gulladuff; I was on the move again. I came outside and made the call from the car phone as I was driving towards Maghera. He answered. I said who I was and the phone went dead - I had gone into one of the many blank spots that lie along this road. I tried again further down the road, this time pulling in to the side of the road to make sure it didn't happen again. This time I said, 'it's me again', and asked if he wanted to meet me. 'Yes,' he said. I said I would be at the side of the pub in Gulladuff within twenty minutes and that if he wasn't there, I would be gone - total arrogance, but at the moment that's me. Before he had a chance to reply, I hung up.

I arrived within ten minutes of our phone call and sat on a wall opposite the pub. This gave me a good vantage point to watch anyone coming without them being aware of me. He arrived within the twenty minutes. I suggested that we go to Maghera and get a cup of tea; he invited me to go to his house. His wife (Mena is her name) answered the door and I am sure she didn't know what to think of this character who had only announced his coming less than half an hour before.

Fr Frank had said that when he met Patsy, he knew he was my brother, but I must honestly say that I didn't see any great resemblance between us (except the chin area, and how many people have similar chins?); even his colouring was different. He has three daughters and a son. Two of the girls have auburn hair and the third is the child of Sally's dreams: a beautiful wee girl with red curly hair.

Paddy, as he is known in Gulladuff, is an electrician by trade. I feel he was - and I don't blame him - being protective of those in Draperstown.

No one knows anything, is what he is saying. He offered to take me round, show me the area and introduce me to the cousins as his friend.

'Hold it,' I said. 'If I ever go into any of these places or meet them - and I don't even know if I want to - I will go as Johnny McCallion; Rose Kelly's birth son. I have been hidden away for too long.'

I told him how I'd felt when I heard of Jimmy's visits and that I hoped I didn't sound too ungrateful but, as I said, that's me at the moment. He refers to her as 'Granny Rose'. He talked a lot of his earlier days and how 'Da' Kelly (his grandfather) meant so much to him growing up. He talked of the times Rose came to visit and how he had asked her to buy him something, and she asked him why should she?

'Because you are my mother,' he said. Rose asked him who had told him that. Aunt Tessie, was his reply. Rose and Tessie both laughed at this. So the lies out of Draperstown are starting to fall apart: Fr Frank had been told they had lost all contact with Rose for over ten years but how could this have been the case if Patsy was able to talk of all the visits she had made when he was young?

Patsy also talked of the times he went to Belfast and how she had worked as a waitress in the Continental Café. In the late fifties, I went to Windsor Park to watch an international and I am fairly sure that's the café I ate in before the match. I wonder did she serve me there. Just as with Jimmy, I seemed to know more about the family background than Patsy did. But then, I reason to ask about when her brothers and sisters were born - even those who died in infancy.

He talked of how he and Da Kelly would journey into Draperstown on a Friday to buy leather for repairing the shoes. So Da was a shoemaker, just like my Daddy; another coincidence or what? I am sure there are many more things to discover but I will take my time. I had to leave for home then, but I am sure we will meet again. Another piece of the jigsaw is in place.

* * * * *

Tuesday, July 9th

The writing of the book continues.

* * * * *

Wednesday, July 10th

I feel so wracked with guilt; 'betrayal' is the word that would describe it best. Betrayal of someone who I love so much, and I just wonder does he even know. Today, I decided I had to go to him. Of course, I am talking of my brother, Kevin. Of all the journeys I have made to date, this is the most difficult because he - and only he - is my brother; my God had planned it that way from the beginning. As I suspected, he joked about it all from the beginning as I slowly told my tale.

His children came in during this time looking for their tea and they were given the money to go to the chip shop and not to be in too big a hurry to come back. Kevin joked that I might have a claim on land over there and asked what that made *him* to them all, saying, 'I am your man's "let's go claim it all"'.

At one point, he said, 'so you have a brother in Gulladuff'.

I shot straight back at him, 'I have only one brother and he is here'.

He said, 'ach, you know what I mean', or something like that.

After I had revealed the existence of the girl and the fella in England, he made another one of his smart comments and I thought, *I will sort you out shortly.*

When he thought that was everything, he said, 'that's some story'.

I said: 'That's not all, for another boy was born in 1953 and had been adopted and reared by a family in Coleraine, and I had a phone call from him earlier today asking for advice on how to build barricades (at this time the Protestants were putting up blockades in the north of Ireland) because he and his friends had no experience in these things.'

You see, in the midst of such a serious situation, I can still laugh at life.

Kevin looked at me in disbelief and said, 'I knew you were going to do something like this to me: you are not only telling me he is a bastard - just like us - but that he is a Protestant bastard into the bargain!'

We laughed and joked about all of this. He asked me if I would advise him to go on a search like this and I said only if he had worked out the worst possible scenario and had decided that he could cope with it.

Then, and only then, should he take that step. Kevin laughingly said, 'you have already revealed that one'.

I then said if he did this and expected the worst, then everything else would be a bonus. 'But Kevin,' I warned, 'still be prepared for the knockbacks.'

I hope I didn't hurt you, Kevin. I love you so much.

I Am In Focus Again

Thursday, July 11th

The journey continues and the urgency is on the move again. I must find out where she is buried. Fr Frank must be on his holidays because I rang him on Tuesday and Wednesday but no one answered and today (I was doing a call for work nearby) I called at his house and there was no sign of life. So where do I go from here? That's the question.

On a lighter note, I passed the new graveyard over at Brackaghlislea today and found the graves of Rose's sisters, Alice and Josephine, and her brother Patrick.

They all died at what I would consider young enough ages. Alice was the oldest of them and she was only 66 years old. I joked with Sally later on that I must go on a search of my natural father to see if it increases my chances for a longer life.

Back to the serious side: as I stood by the side of Alice's grave, my eyes filled with tears and then they flowed down my cheeks freely. She, I felt, was the one lady who would have told me the truth.

This was the Kelly who would have accepted me for who I am and who would not have denied my very existence. This is what I feel. They are robbing me of the right to be totally me. But enough of them for now.

I have a mission and I am in danger of losing sight of it. I need to find out where Rose is buried.

A thought struck me that if I made contact with the priest in charge of the Catholic church in Filey I might get lucky. So I rang enquiries and I experienced another one of my shots in the dark (or are they?) paying off again.

The operator gave her name, asked if she could help me and which number I wanted. I replied, 'I hope you can; I don't even know who I am looking for'. I went on to explain that I was looking for a Catholic church in a wee place called Filey, in West Yorkshire.

Now, remember when you ring the operator these days you can get anyone in the British Isles. This was her reply: 'Ever heard of it? I go there every year on my holiday - in fact, I am going there this Saturday. You are looking for St Mary's and the number is 01723 513139.'

I asked if she knew the priest's name (she didn't). But two out of three's not bad, is it? I left a message on the answering machine (oh God, I hate these contraptions). Fr Sean O'Donnell is the priest's name. I tried to explain the purpose of my call and then the tape ran out. I hope my luck hasn't.

On Thursday nights, for the past four weeks, a group of us has been meeting, in the presence of the Blessed Sacrament, to pray for the success of the pilgrimage walk to Knock.

Tonight, as I thanked the group who had organised tonight's hour of prayer, I said that I personally had found this hour in the oratory to be a harbour of peace throughout this time of turmoil, for this is what it has been.

It has sustained me, it has carried me and it has protected me and freed me from many of the things that would have burdened me. Thank you, Jesus, for your promise to be with me always, especially in this special way in your Eucharistic presence. Don't ever let me turn my back on you, Lord.

* * * * *

Friday, July 12th

Fr O'Donnell returned my call and apologised for not ringing last night, as it was after ten before he got home. I explained what I was looking for and how I needed his help.

I told him of Ted and Kathleen (John, too, lived in Filey, but he was currently working away on the oil rigs) but explained I didn't want them alerted to my request as I don't know if I will ever go near them; they aren't really part of my quest.

He said he would check the records as it all happened before he came there. He may even have to go to the local undertakers. He will get back to me as soon as he can.

Today my heart is saddened with the news that my good friend Eric Mullane has died. Another part of the letting go. Nancy explained to Sally that he had died on Tuesday last in Coleraine hospital, but because of the situation in that area, they were unable to bring his remains home (the North is in turmoil again). When will we ever learn to live with each other in peace?

Rather than put pressure on people like myself who would have had to travel, the family decided to wait until after the funeral before contacting us. I thank the Lord for the privilege that was mine to be able to count him among my friends. He was certainly one of the people who has made me what I am today. Be gentle, Lord, with Nancy and their children; she, in particular, has been giving all of her life - or for as long as I have known her, anyway.

* * * * *

Saturday, July 13th

I paid my last respects to my friend Eric. Nancy was surprised that I had been able to find his grave. If only she knew. This has been a disastrous week for the North. Never before have we had so much need of prayer, wisdom and reconciliation. God help us to love; sometimes it can be so hard.

* * * * *

Sunday, July 14th

Today, Edna asked me to do the pilgrimage walk for myself. Maybe I will; then again, maybe I won't.

* * * * *

Monday, July 15th

Fr O'Donnell rang. He has gone directly to Ted Cappelman and spoken to him. While nothing directly was said, he feels that the door is opening and that Ted knows more than he is saying just now. Fr O'Donnell said that he sensed the great love Ted had for Rose because of the way he spoke of her.

The coincidences continue. Kathleen Kelly, who is married now and called Coultas, works at a hospitality home run by a Sr Eileen (from Belfast, I think he said). She has a son called David who is getting married in St Mary's on October 12th. He also said that Rose died on January 4th, 1980, not January 6th; I wonder will that crowd in Draperstown get anything right? Anyway, he still hasn't gotten the information regarding her grave. I've said I will ring him next week.

I got angry with God today about Emmet's situation - and not just about baby Kevin, who was suddenly taken into hospital. He has had enough crap in his young life.

It's now time for a break, Lord. Baby Kevin came home from the hospital today. Thanks be to God, for that part of the prayer being answered; now for the rest.

*****

Tuesday, July 16th

Today I awoke with tears in my eyes. Why? At last, someone near her might just know and share something they know with me. I don't know why, but the panic is back again.

I just feel that I must get away from it all and collect myself because I am in great danger of letting down my guard and showing the world how I feel; broken dreams and all of that. I just wonder, at times, what or who do people see when they look at me? This man of God, full of strength in the Lord.

Don't be fooled by me; please don't be fooled by the mask that I wear (masks, in fact). Look for and find the little boy who hurts, despite all the good things he has enjoyed in life.

He still hurts deep, deep down, in the very depth of his being where he doesn't let anyone go - not even the man he is today, though they must meet and sort all this out.

It is not about Rose Kelly now but about Johnny McCallion and Johnny Kelly and what they have in common: hurt, rejection and fear of the unknown.

Thank God for Sally. I wonder what she feels sometimes. Someday, Sally, we must talk about what you think of it all. I always want you to listen; maybe I should listen for a change.

Thank you, Lord, for Johnnie White and for the peace and tranquillity I found as I walked with him and talked with him on Fahan beach. Time out; time to think. Tomorrow, we head for Knock and all that it holds.

Our Spirits Meet

Wednesday, July 17th

The main theme of the pilgrimage walk is 'peace' - in our hearts, in our homes, and in our country. At this time, we need to pray so much for all of that. In addition, we all bring our own petitions with us. Mine is centred on my family; my whole family. This year's involvement by me in the walk very much reflects my life in general at this time - being called on a road that I wouldn't choose to travel of my own free will.

The organisers have asked me to lead the liturgy, which means I will have to organise things like readers, music and bidding prayers, among other things.

I want to walk but I know by now my God has never got it wrong yet, so I will follow. I will walk whenever I can and pray wherever I am. That is His will.

We start this pilgrimage with Mass in St Eugene's Cathedral and it will end with Mass in the old chapel in Knock on Sunday afternoon. We will have walked the road of life together and shared in its pain and joys, and maybe we will have come a little closer to God the Father, through Jesus and Mary.

My prayer for all concerned is that we can leave the baggage of life at the Eucharistic tables we will meet at over the next few days, as it will be a difficult enough journey even if we travel light.

$$* * * * *$$

Friday, July 19th

Our Mary's birthday. It has extra special significance for me this year as it coincides with the healing Mass, which is always held on the Friday of the pilgrimage. It is the only Mass that isn't said in a church used every day by the local congregation. Fr Pat always asked us to prepare in advance for this one. As we journey throughout Friday by whatever mode of transport (driven or on foot) we pray as we go, calling on all the angels and saints of God to surround us at this time and protect us from all that isn't of God.

I had very much been enjoying my involvement in the music ministry (I don't know if others had, but that is their problem).

When the Mass was about to start, I left my guitar on the ground because I realised that, if I didn't, I wouldn't be tuned into what God was trying to do for me.

Just then, Fr Pat called on all the angels and saints and the souls of our departed relatives and ancestors to surround us and protect us.

It was then that I got the feeling of her presence for the first time since this journey began. But the little boy wants set free; he wants to know why was he rejected.

And he wants to show his hurt. At last, the man and the little boy have met and both are hurting, because all we ever wanted was five minutes with her, just to say we love her and to feel her arms around us. Rose, there are no questions; just love.

At last, the dam has broken. The boom has burst and the tears that I have held back are flowing freely. It's now just me. *Why? Why? Why?*

Sally says I must accept that I won't see her in this life, but I ask her (Rose), if she is present, just to blow on me. In a church, on a very warm summer evening, that is something that may have seemed impossible, but the God I believe in can do anything.

I know that she was there because blow she did. That's me for today; to bed content in the Lord I go.

* * * * *

Saturday, July 20th

This is our Catherine's birthday. God gifted Sally and me with two daughters, born almost ten years apart. I got a few lessons in humility today because I planned my day only to find God had other plans for me.

Firstly, I always said that we must lead by example. Well, I went to get my big toe dressed (it was chafing from all the walking) so that I could walk, but the medics said, 'no way, Johnny; not today you won't. Let's see tomorrow'.

My mood is foul, to put it mildly. I just seem to be a passenger this year. Kevin Glackin says to me, 'so you're in a "poor me" mood'.

'Why not,' says I, 'haven't I got plenty of reason to be? Nothing is ever the way I want it.'

Just then, someone came to me and said they were having a bit of bother convincing a young person to take a lift up into the middle of the crowd. Over I goes to talk to them (in love, I hope) about the dangers of pride and the need to be humble at this time. See how quickly I can put on the mask; great hypocrite! The thought that struck me then (in the silence, of course) was, listen to what you are saying and practise what you preach. My God speaking to me again.

Then, at the evening celebration of Mass, I was asked to reflect on the gifts from guidelines I had been given. I spoke about what we had all been through these last few days as pilgrims.

The first gift was flowers, representing the joys we have shared - despite my moods.

Secondly, the cross, symbolising the crucifixion of many, as we walked in pain and hope, held down with the weight of our petitions and maybe not allowing others to help us on our way. Even Jesus let Simon help him; another example (one of many) of how we can humble ourselves.

Thirdly, the stole, representing the Sacraments, of which we have been gifted with many: we have had Eucharist, we have had reconciliation and we have had the anointing at the healing in Friday's Mass. Why am I moaning when I have been given so many graces? They have been flowing as freely as the tears of Friday evening.

* * * * *

Sunday, July 21st

The final journey, and I am ready. Am I what? I so wanted to get out on the road on my own (alone, my God, with thee) but, again, that was not to be, as my God knew better: he sent Danny Blee and Thomas Gallagher to walk by my side. A few miles from Knock, I waited for Sally to join me; how she is suffering from the physical strains of the walk.

We walk together into Knock to be met by a group of young people, including our own Mary. It's great to hold her in my arms. These are the people who give me the strength to carry on. And then it was home, to Derry, to bed and rest... but for how long? That is the question.

* * * * *

Monday, July 22nd

A day of rest in the Lord. I pray that Sally's pain is soon eased. She really is a great warrior for her God. She drives herself to extremes and I pray that he grants her petitions.

Someone Must Know

Tuesday, July 23rd

I phoned Fr O'Donnell in Filey. Still no word on Rose's grave and the agitation is back. Someone somewhere must know. Then I remembered that Patsy was one of the three who had gone over at the time of her death; maybe he will remember something. I rang him. He can't remember very much about the graveyard or its name, because as he said (understandably so) he was too upset at the time and had only arrived the night before her funeral. Kathleen had insisted he travel in the family car and the rest of them travelled in other cars. Something was wrong: someone had told Fr Frank that only Patsy, Alice and her niece had gone to the funeral and that no contact had been made with Kathleen and John. So, me being me, I asked Patsy who was over from Draperstown for the funeral and he named the whole seed, breed and generation.

Again, I asked myself: *Why? Why? Why?* All I ever wanted was the truth, and this they have denied me; to protect their name, their reputation and their faces. They will never know the hurt they have caused me. My gut feelings have proved once again to be right and I am so angry and hurt. I want to hurt them, but how? I will write this book and change every name in it except theirs (I know I won't, but for now it makes me feel better).

Wednesday, July 24th

I phoned Fr Frank to tell him of all that had unfolded and Sally phoned the records offices in Filey and Scarborough to see if we could get any information regarding Rose's burial place ourselves. I think I must be the most impatient person ever born.

* * * * *

Saturday, July 27th

I left Jimmy over the copies of everything I had promised him. He wasn't at home. It gave me a chance to ask Edith how he has been since I came out of the woodwork. She said he has been on cloud nine. If only I could feel the same. In truth, I am struggling with this new idea of these new-found 'brothers and sister', as people keep referring to them. But I feel in a bit better form today.

* * * * *

Sunday, July 28th

The clouds have descended on me again. I was in good form so I don't know why I suddenly felt the way I did. The agitation is driving me and I can't rest. I just have to get out of the house. Sally (that great lady) caught on very quickly and said she would go with me if I wanted her to. We went to Lisfannon beach and walked. As we did, I got to thinking of going to Filey, but said if it was leaving me feeling like this, maybe I should drop the idea until a later time because Sally didn't need

129

this during her holidays. She said I should go - get it over with and then get on with life. Even Sally, my great guardian, doesn't understand. But then, how could she, because at times neither do I. I now know that no one can get inside my mind or my heart to feel what I feel about it all.

* * * * *

Monday, July 29th

Today I took myself back to Draperstown. How I hate imposing on Fr Frank and Marie, both of whom have been pillars of strength and support for me throughout this time. When I arrived, I said: 'Father, I don't even know why I am here. You asked me to take my time and work out what it would take to help me on this journey. I still don't know.'

I explained that I felt my visits to Draperstown were fast coming to an end because there is nothing left here for me anymore. I don't mean I won't be visiting Fr Frank, because I can never ever thank him and Marie for all they have done for me. I may have to use him as a buffer on a few occasions yet, when the dark clouds of despair move in again, as I am sure they will. While we were chatting, Fr Frank said, 'Johnny, I think there is something you are still not asking'. Johnnie White (he who doesn't even know how to spell his own Christian name, but I will humour him this one time) had said the same thing to me recently. If only I could figure out what. Father said he may approach his contact again to test out the ground and see if there is any change in the situation. I don't know if it will do any good.

Still no word of my Wild Irish Rose's resting place. It was when walking to Knock I decided to refer to her by this term of endearment. It's as near as I can go to calling her 'mother'.

* * * * *

Tuesday, July 30th

The agitation is back. No one knows how I feel when this happens; I must do something. I rang Sally around 2pm and asked her if any word had come in the post in connection with the grave. Nothing had. She rang back at 2.15pm to say they had confirmed her last resting place: it is at St Oswald's cemetery in Filey; they are sending a plan. The one thing that maybe, deep down, I had been hoping wasn't true has now been confirmed. Rose is dead. So, they can tell the truth at times.

Sally asked me if I was OK. I didn't know but said I was. She asked me again; this time I said I needed to contact Kathleen in England - but how? I didn't have her address or phone number, so back to shooting in the dark again. Around tea time, I phoned enquiries again, hoping I would get a lucky break... and I did. There were only two Coultases listed in Filey: one was ex-directory and the other was a K Coultas.

'Of West Road?' I asked, as this was Ted Cappelman's address.

'No,' came the reply. I think she said Ashgrove, so I decided to take that number.

So now I have a number. What do I do? This could be anyone. So I rang Fr Sean O'Donnell and asked if he could confirm that I had the right details. He said I did.

'What are you going to do now?' he asked.

'I don't know,' was my reply. Sounds familiar, doesn't it?

'I will pray that you make the right decision,' Fr Sean answered.

I knew he was right because the decisions have all had to be mine since I took control of my life. Around 8.30pm, I made the phone call. I had walked up and down the hallway like a cat on a hot tin roof for a few hours. A woman answered (her daughter, as it turned out) and I asked to speak to Kathleen. After what seemed like an eternity, Kathleen came to the phone. I don't really remember how that call started, except that I asked her to sit down as I had something to say which may come as a shock. I immediately explained that it wasn't anything to worry about.

At this stage, she asked who was speaking. I explained that my name wouldn't mean anything to her but asked did the name Rose Kelly mean anything to her?

'She's my mum,' came the reply.

I said: 'And according to my investigations, she is my birth mother'.

'Oh my God, who is speaking?' she asked.

I told her my name was Johnny McCallion and explained that I had been born John Joseph Kelly.

'Oh my God,' she said again. 'Don't blame my mum - she didn't let you go easily - don't blame my mum.'

I tried to explain that my journey was not about blame, but rather to tell Rose Kelly that I was OK and that I had to thank her for the gift of life she had given me.

Kathleen then asked: 'Where have you been and how have you been?'

I told her not to worry about me, that I was OK and had been greatly loved and was very happy. She asked me what age I was. I told her (53), and then discovered she was less than two years younger than me. She then said she had much to tell me.

Her next question threw me for a second: 'Has it been you who has been checking out mum's grave?'

I said it was, but how did she know that? It turns out some friend of hers works in the office we had been phoning and had told her. I explained that I did not want to cause upset to anyone - least of all did I want to cause any hurt to Rose's reputation as I didn't know if anyone knew of me.

Then she asked if I was coming to Filey and if I was, I would have to stay with Ted Cappelman - if I agreed to her telling him, that is. I said she could tell him but that we would be staying in a guest house as we didn't want to inconvenience anyone and that she didn't have the right to assume that he would want to put us up.

She went on to say that he came round to her for dinner three or four times every week. He must mean something to her after all these years.

After she absorbed the opening shockwaves of who I was, Kathleen made me feel very welcome; at last, someone in the Kelly connection was. That might sound very unfair with regards to Jimmy and Patsy - both of whom welcomed me with open arms - but maybe the difference this time was the fact that I wanted to feel this way.

We talked at length and she said she had a lot to tell me and that there was a lot she wanted to hear. So here we go on our way again.

Earlier this evening, Sally asked me if I was sorry that I had started this quest. I said I wasn't. Strangely, she said she was because of how it was affecting me. I had to stop her going on a guilt trip there and then (aren't I the master of those?) because she had encouraged me to start. I told her that I wouldn't change anything, despite the pain, because I now know more about myself and that was important to me. I hope I have allayed her fears. Later on, I phoned Fr Frank to tell him the news and he was delighted that I had got good news at last. But really, in a strange way, it has all been good news.

* * * * *

Wednesday, July 31st

'At peace at last' is how I would describe my feelings; with the world and with myself. Looking back once again on the last ten weeks, I am reminded of something I had said to Sally yesterday when I was trying to put her mind at ease. It shocked me because it summed it all up.

'Sally' I'd said, 'I have had to pack 53 years of living into these last ten weeks; in fact, I have had to live a lifetime.'

The enormity of that hadn't really sunk in. I have been on the roller coaster of life, just like those people who talk of having an experience where their lives passed before them in seconds. In my own way, I was going through this and still having to get on with everyday living as well. *Thank God for God,* I say again, otherwise I would have cracked up. I thank Him for these human angels of life that He sent to surround me at this time: my family and friends; companions on a journey.

I don't need Draperstown anymore; not getting to know me is their loss. My self-esteem is on the way up again because I know who I am.

I phoned Fr O'Donnell to tell him of all that had happened since we spoke yesterday - that's if he doesn't already know. In fact, he did, as Kathleen had called with him and told him that she was shocked with the suddenness of it all but delighted that I had had the courage to ring her. He said she had told him she felt I was the one most hurt in all of this. Maybe I am... maybe I am.

* * * * *

Thursday, August 1st

I decided to ring Kathleen because I don't know what upset or turmoil I may have caused her on Tuesday when I rang her out of the blue. She wasn't at home but her husband was. He too is called John, and he told me that she was shaken but was now coming to terms with it all. John said that Kathleen had told Ted Cappleman but that he didn't know anything; Rose hadn't told him of me. Again, I asked what was going on. 'Doesn't anyone know of me? Am I really Mr Nobody and didn't she tell anyone of me at all?' Sally reminded me about a young girl who had recently given birth to a set of twins. Up until the day before they were born she had told her friends that she definitely wasn't pregnant. So maybe Rose didn't tell anyone, either; but I still don't know.

* * * * *

Saturday, August 3rd

It really was a beautiful day so we decided to have a barbecue. Mammy and Daddy came down and all of the others gathered as well. Around half-seven, Kathleen rang and I said if there was an awkwardness regarding Ted that we could book into a guest house, but she said no way. She said he hadn't slept the night she had told him of me as he hadn't been aware of my existence. But then, who is, anyway? He is trying to put some stuff, like photographs of her, together to show me. It's great to find people who are open enough to talk to me of her and not just avoid me. She also said she had phoned her brother John and that he would like to meet me if that would be OK.

I asked her how her children were regarding the news; she said they were grand. I warned her to be careful after my own experience with Mary, who hadn't liked the idea of me contacting 'that man Jimmy'. But, as I pointed out to her, I was 'that man Johnny' to Jimmy's children. I hope that did the trick. I told Kathleen that I had asked my Wild Irish Rose what was going on. Kathleen said that she had gone to her grave and asked her the same question today. She was so concerned for me and what had happened to me. I assured her that I was wrapped in cotton wool and cosseted with so much love since I came to Mammy and Daddy - and especially by Sally since we had got married.

She said that Rose hadn't given me up easily and I said that I already knew that from the story that had unfolded so far. She talked about the pain I must have come through as I made this journey and as I head to Filey. I told her I had gone over every possible scenario with that one, and that, yes, there was pain and there would possibly be more to come. But I had to go through with it; had to complete my mission. She asked about Sally and said she must be something special... isn't she that, and more?

The Final Journey

Monday, August 5th

Today, the final journey begins. We leave Derry for Cork, and from there (via Dublin) to England and all that it holds. I cried yesterday as I left Mammy and Daddy; if only I could tell them what I am about, but I can't at the moment.

My feelings are mixed just now and I hope I don't take away from Sally's and Mary's holidays. We drove from Derry to Cork in the pouring rain to stay with Catherine and Pat until Wednesday, and then to Dublin.

* * * * *

Tuesday, August 6th

I awoke very early this morning trying to capture the holiday spirit. We went into Cork to buy a present for Kathleen and Ted, and as I walked around the store, my eyes just filled with tears. I should be buying something for my Wild Irish Rose... just let me out; set me free!

* * * * *

Wednesday, August 7th

So today has come. As I walked along the seafront with Deefer (our Yorkshire terrier - some irony that!) I let things mull around in my mind. Firstly, we will be leaving Catherine and Pat, then heading to Dublin and on to England. Maybe I will find the answers. Maybe there I will come to know why I have been brought on this journey, because, even now, I know I didn't make a deliberate choice at the outset to come along this road. Though, later on, I certainly made decisions to continue and to push ahead with it all.

I, who normally has no bother expressing my feelings, am at this time having great difficulty in doing so. I fear all that lies ahead. How will we all react to each other? How will I react when I go to her grave? How will I ever leave her? *How?* But leave her I must. This journey has been made possible because of the support I have received in abundance from all of you around me; with your unconditional love.

Please, just bear with me a little longer and all will be well again. In fact, all will be better, in God's time. I hope Rose doesn't fear my coming and that I haven't hurt her in any way during my search. Take care of Sally and Mary, Lord, as You have always done, as they make this journey, which isn't really theirs, with me.

* * * * *

Thursday, August 8th

It really is difficult to put into words how I feel just now. The emotions are running the gamut. The quest is reaching an end. *Or is it?* Only time will tell. There is so much to fear and still so much to hope for. My moods are swinging from guilt and despair to joy and elation. I remember, as the boat neared Holyhead, I said to Sally, 'let's head straight to Emmet, Edna, Marie and Kevin in Plymouth and phone Filey and tell them that we will see them some other time', and, believe me, that's how I felt.

All the panic and fear have returned along with the dread of what lies ahead. I just want to be with all of mine so that I can feel secure and safe again, but I know that I must go into the unknown so that it can be revealed, faced and conquered. Dear Lord, be with me always. We made the journey mostly in daylight, arriving in Filey just as darkness descended. At last, we are here. 'Apprehensive' is just one of the many words I can think of to describe my feelings at this time. I wonder what Kathleen's are.

Part of me is saying that this is so unreal it's unbelievable; that it isn't really happening. I hope I will wake up soon and be the same, uncomplicated Johnny McCallion that I have always been... but I know I won't.

I don't remember knocking at her door. I don't remember who answered; her husband or her daughter. I don't, but there, standing in the centre of the living room, was this woman who had opened her door and home to me, a stranger, along with Sally and Mary. We could have been con artists, but we weren't. I wondered again, *how does she feel?* She isn't anything like I imagined. She isn't in the least like me. Am I in the right place? But the child within me won't take no for an answer; he wants to press on. This is his time; this is his journey. He must know all that is to be known. The man is willing to accept all in faith, but the child wants to put his fingers and hands into the wounds so that he can be at peace. *He hears you, kid. Go for it: now really is your time.*

And so the child asks: *Did she tell them of me? Did she say why she let me go? Did she regret it or didn't she care? Why, as Kathleen says, was I the one who was hurt most of all?*

All this, and more, he wants to know. There is only one disappointment in store, because what is unfolding now is that she hasn't told anyone of me (not even Ted Cappelman) but all of them are willing to talk openly of Rose. Kath, as they call her over here, keeps apologising for 'Mum' (as she calls my Wild Irish Rose) for all of the hurt she feels I was caused. But as the night unfolds, I have my earlier feelings confirmed: it wasn't me who suffered most.

She told me of Rose's struggle to keep her and John together in Belfast. She had to go out to work and so left them in the care of others - not always a wise thing to do, but then, necessity must. How they had slept in one room in a house that was owned by a woman, Ma Gorman, who seemed to foster or look after a lot of children. Rose was very much ruled by this person, is the conclusion I have come to, and I don't think I like what I sense.

Kath spoke of Rose going to work for a few summers in Filey and of her having left them in Belfast. I suppose it was during this time that she met Ted; I never thought to ask that one.

She talked of her love for a lady who, once again, seems to keep popping up in this quest of mine: Alice Kelly. One of Rose's older sisters, she and her boyfriend Andy had been a great support to them all at that time. For some reason, Kath seems to think that John's father is also mine.

His name was John Ward: a Protestant, so they couldn't marry because of the situation in the North. He worked in the abattoir in the market area of Belfast. She recalled how Rose would often call him 'Johnny' and how she felt that Rose didn't let me go easily.

Then she told me how she felt when I walked through the door. I recall her saying over and over, 'I don't believe this. Oh my God, I don't believe this'.

What didn't she believe? That I was here, or what? She went on to explain that it was as if a light had gone on as I'd walked into the room and any doubts she may have had just went.

If she had half as many as I have at this moment, then she has plenty. She said it was because her brother John and I were the image of each other. *She is grasping at straws,* I was thinking at that instant. *What the hell, and why am I here?*

Everyone was saying how alike John and I are - including John's wife, who had also arrived by then. But John hadn't come with her and I wonder what was going on in his head at this time. After all, I am the one who bears the name he has been given. *Why did she give him my name? Wasn't he good enough to have his own name?* I am sure that even I can't touch in on his thoughts. We didn't meet tonight. Maybe we will tomorrow; maybe we won't.

Kath told us how they came over to Filey when she was nine and how Rose married Ted in the registry office. The local Catholic priest couldn't marry them in the church as Ted had been married before and his wife was still alive then. Rose had helped out in the summertime at one of the local shorefront stalls; she eventually took it over and ran it herself. It also unfolded that she would have helped anyone in need; she'd been there often enough herself. Apparently, she finally learned to drive and passed her test after many attempts. She was, as we say, a 'hard goer'.

Then Kath spoke of how Rose took ill with cancer and how she came off work to look after her mum and care for her through her illness, and how Rose asked Kath why, in spite of all of her caring, Kath couldn't show her love.

Again, I am crying inside, Lord; why do you do this to me? She talked of the final days and hours of Rose's illness and her struggle to cling onto life, and how she called out, 'they are coming to get me'. Kath didn't know what she meant, but maybe I did. 'They', I feel, were Jimmy and me. Oh my God, I hope it wasn't too painful for her. The words of Sr Bernadine now mean so much more. She had asked me if I ever thought of Rose's pain at not having me and Jimmy there when she was dying. I hadn't.

Kath talked of how her son Patrick was close to Rose and how he got a feeling around 10 o'clock that evening that something was wrong. It was at 10pm on January 4th, 1980, that she died in hospital in Hull. I don't know how I feel. Numbness, detachment and remoteness, I suppose. Outside of it all. It has nothing to do with me. But why, oh why, didn't she tell anyone of me? Didn't she care? Oh, how angry and hurt I am over this; not even one person seems to know of me. It's as if I never existed, as if the child of her womb never was. But he did and I am, so we will claim our rightful place in all of this.

Luckily, we have been surrounded by so much love all of our lives. As Johnny McCallion, again I pray for those who make this journey into their origins (or try to make it) in the belief that what they will find will change their lives for the better. They will need great strength and depth of being to be able to do so.

* * * * *

Friday, August 9th

I spoke to Ted this morning, but nothing of any great importance has been revealed. Rose hadn't told him of me. I just wonder how she kept it to herself. Was she so unsure of his love for her? Did she do it to protect John and Kath from the kind of life they must have had in Belfast before she met Ted? I don't know.

We went to Kath's for our breakfast. Oh, how nervous she is, apologising for her mum. I tell her again that it is neither her place nor duty to do this, as only Rose can tell us why I had to go. I signalled to Sally to leave us alone so that Kath and I could talk freely. You see, I knew, from the dates she mentioned last night and the way she was talking, that she thought I must be the young child (who was actually Jimmy) from the days in Belfast when she and John lived with Rose in Ma Gorman's boarding house.

Sally and I discussed the situation last night after we realised that Rose hadn't told anyone about him, either. I knew if I didn't, I would be doing to him what has been done to me: I would be denying him his right to be known. Kath began by saying how sorry she was that she couldn't fill me in with more information about myself. I pointed out again that I am very secure, and have always been, because of the love I have been given, as Johnny McCallion, by all.

We started to talk again of their lives in Belfast. I will not discuss the details of that conversation but will simply say she confirmed my concerns from last night that life had not been easy for her. It turns out I wasn't the one most hurt after all.

I said that only Jesus could heal us all and that we needed to put ourselves safely in His hands, by going to Him in the Sacraments of true healing - reconciliation and Eucharist - as often as we can. We talked of this for I don't know how long. I now know that my God brought me to Filey not just to go to Rose but also to meet Kath. I hope and pray that I have fulfilled His mission for me - in His way and not mine.

I told her that my journey had taken me along a strange road and that I had, out of necessity, uncovered many facts relating to Rose. I explained I had a document relating to the adoption of one James K Kelly, in 1956, on which I had seen the signature of Rose Bridget Kelly. I could only suppose it was hers, but Kath could confirm or deny it for sure. She was shocked, I am sure, but there really wasn't any easy way for me to handle this one. I then produced the document and showed it to her. She confirmed it was Rose's signature: Jimmy is her son.

Kath couldn't understand how, at nine years of age, she wouldn't have been aware that Jimmy (who would have been a baby) was her little brother. But, I said, given that it was a house owned by a woman who took in foster children, there would have been many children coming and going; what was another one?

'Then how didn't I know she was pregnant?' she said.

'A nine-year-old back in the fifties was not as aware of the facts of life as a nine-year-old would be today,' I said.

We talked at length about the parentage of each of us and she seems to believe that John's and her father could also be mine and that Patsy's and Jimmy's fathers are different men. I don't have any tangible proof of this, and to be honest, I don't think it matters so much to me.

Sally re-joined us and Kath told us how Rose took her back to Draperstown once, on a day visit, and when someone asked who she was, Rose replied: 'She is the daughter of my next-door-neighbour in Filey and we brought her with us on holiday to Ireland.' Kath talked at length about her feelings of hurt caused by what she saw (and rightly so) as the ultimate denial by Rose. Kath said that she felt so rejected.

At this time, Alice was living in Belfast, and when she returned there that evening she cried and cried as she asked Alice, 'why did Mum do this to me?' I don't remember if she told me what Alice said in reply; one day I will ask her.

She went on to talk of how good Ted was (and still is) to them, and of the summers Rose had come to work in Filey (before they had come over there to live) and how she had left them with Ma Gorman and how alone she felt then. As I said, I wasn't the one who was most hurt in all of this. We talked about a lot of things this morning, but the one thing we seemed to avoid was the purpose of my being here: to visit Rose's grave. Eventually, I said it was time for me to go there and Kath said she would go with me.

'No,' I said. 'This is my journey; mine, and mine alone.' I hope I didn't hurt her, but it is.

We wandered through the town and then to the cemetery. Kath left me there, having arranged to meet up with the others for a cup of tea in Filey. I said I didn't know how long I would be. I just asked for time and space.

Mission Complete

Friday, August 9th (continued)

Cemeteries seem to be central to my mission. They have held so many links from my past and here was the ultimate one. Here, in front of me now, lay the lady who had given me the gift of life. In this foreign land lay my past; the goal of my journey. Here lay the lady with all the answers; but would she give them to me? I didn't know.

At last, my goal was in sight. I had brought five red roses for my Wild Irish Rose: one for each decade we'd been apart. The numbness and feeling of remoteness had returned. I had, at last, caught up with her: the running was over and the hunt had ended. I had come as close in this life as I ever could to her. I just sank to the ground, not able to think. I couldn't even shed a tear, my emotions under control, as usual. When would I ever let go? *When, when, when?*

I couldn't yet cry because I knew, beyond doubt, that I hadn't come to bury her. I still didn't fully know her and that was going to take time. After a long time of silence, I began by asking her was there really no one that she told of me?

Is there no one who knows of me, and if not, why not?

I told her I had found this the hardest thing to accept: not that I am adopted (that has never been a problem) or that she let me go; but the fact that no one seems to know of me. Why didn't she acknowledge me to the world? *Why?* I didn't get any answers to this one. I told her of Mammy and Daddy, about how much love and affection they had given me over the years and how I wouldn't change them, or anything I have had from them, for the world. I told her everything was alright with me because of them, and how I would have loved her to have met them, for it is they who helped mould me from the child of yesterday into the man of today. I told her of Nuala, Marion, and Kevin, my Ma and Da and all of those who helped rear me in the love of my God. I told her of Edward, Stephen, Emmet, Catherine and Mary - God's gifts to me in this life - and how they owed her a great debt of gratitude for the lives they now know. But, most of all, I told her of the rock upon which I am built: Sally.

And then, the tears flowed freely because I couldn't put my arms around her. I couldn't hear the sound of her voice. I couldn't see the smile on her face nor could I wipe the tears from her eyes. I couldn't hold her hand nor wipe her brow as she lay dying. I couldn't reach her in this world, but as I started running my fingers through the grass on her grave, it took on a different texture - that of hair - and I knew, once again, that what man or woman couldn't do for me, my God did.

The place was engulfed by her presence and I ran my fingers through her hair and I wiped her brow and I wiped her tears. I held her hand in the way my God had shown me because all things are possible to Him in spirit. If only our faith was like the mustard seed: capable, with the right nurturing, of growing to a great size. Time moved on and I knew I was going to have to leave her in this place of the dead and go back to the land of the living. I refused to say goodbye as this was only the beginning. I turned to go several times before I finally did, with tears in my eyes and the question still in my mind, *what was all this about?* Only time will reveal the answer to that one. I must have spent well over an hour and a half with her as it was now 2.30pm.

As I made my way back to the town, I realised it was well over two hours since I had gone to her grave. It was only a ten-minute walk from the cemetery but once I got there I discovered that the living had moved on. How long can you spend over a cup of tea or coffee? I bought myself a battered fish wrapped in newspaper and ate it as I walked through Filey. Again, I found myself in the midst of the crowd but alone with my thoughts - just like the blind man on the road to Jericho. I went to St Mary's to call with Fr Sean O'Donnell but he wasn't at home, so I left a message saying that I had called and that, if I didn't get back, I would contact him when I got back to Derry. Then I headed for Kath's home. I wasn't there very long when the front door opened and in walked John. I knew it was him because I was looking at myself. If I still had any lingering doubts of being in the wrong place, well; his coming has dispelled them. It was as if I was looking in a mirror.

And there was no awkwardness; he spoke of Rose with great love, and why shouldn't he? He has a great respect for Ted and told me how Ted was always there for him and would have been there for me, too. I sensed his regret for what might have been so I reassured him that I had been (and still am) alright where I am and wouldn't change any of that, but that now we had today and the future to build on. He told me of his family and I told him of mine, and we shared a lot of missing years.

After tea time, Sally, Mary and I went for a run down to the seafront. We talked about all that had (or had not) been revealed over the last 24 hours or so. We talked of how I had been blessed over the years and, without actually saying it, how much we loved each other. How or why should I want to change any of my life? On the way back to the car, we decided to call with Fr Sean again; just for a brief visit as we were very tired and feeling very drained at the moment.

Here, I met a truly spiritual man (just as I had hoped) who may be the instrument to bring healing to all of us at a level we have never experienced before. He spoke of his feelings as to why I was on this journey, and of my strength, which he said was based on a deep faith (if we haven't got faith, what do we have?). There was a knock at his sitting room door and I heard a Belfast accent say, 'I have to meet this man', and so entered Sr Eileen... was she some revelation! This journey would not have been complete if I hadn't met her. She spoke of her memories of Kath arriving in Filey, of her starting at the school there, and of how timid she was and how their paths have crossed in these later years. By this time, Fr Sean had gone out to the car and brought Sally and Mary into the house; they didn't want to come in when I came in at the start. He poured a sherry for Sally and me, to toast our meeting, and went on to propose that, in the future when the time was right, he would celebrate a Mass of Healing of the Memories. I knew, then, that he was a man of the Spirit. Thank God for him and bless him all the days of his life. We bade each other farewell.

And so to Kath's. All that she and I talked about that night remains locked in my heart for now. Lord help all young people entrusted into the care of others.

Sally and Mary had headed on round to Ted's and, eventually, I joined them. He showed us many photos of Rose but none of them were any clearer than the one I had at home. He confirmed that they had married in 1957. The fact they had to get married in the registry office and not in the Catholic Church caused Rose real concern, he said, but Fr Rickerly just wouldn't hear of it because Ted was a divorced man. He spoke of her generosity to others and how she never would have asked for anything to be returned that she had loaned to anyone. She was always open to helping anyone in need. I suppose I could have said that that was OK for them, but I didn't. He talked, as Kath did, of her illness, and how, when it was first diagnosed, the consultant had told her that he could cure her, and he did. Then the secondary cancer hit and he couldn't help her that time.

He related how she spent her final Christmas and how, through a Fr Fitzpatrick, she had found peace at last through the healing power of Jesus (my words and thoughts; not Ted's). He shared stories of their visits to Draperstown and how she used to save money on the quiet for those times, and how, when she wanted to get at him, she would say, 'as soon as Kath and John are settled, I am on the first boat back to Belfast'.

The morning after John's wedding, Ted said to Rose as they sat in the kitchen eating their breakfast, 'that money is on top of the fireplace'. What money? she asked. 'Your fare back to Belfast,' said Ted. He laughed as he related this story: you see, she didn't go back to Belfast ever again to stay. All of this is part of me getting to know her, in my way. And so, to bed.

* * * * *

Saturday, August 10th

John was to call up early this morning and we were to go for a walk and a chat along the prom, but, like a lot of other things, it just wasn't meant to be. I got to thinking of Rose and all that Ted had told me regarding their marriage and I just can't help feeling that her struggle was not with Ted, or Fr Rickerly, but in fact with herself, and how, even after all that had happened to her, her faith, and her ability to practise that faith, was indeed very important to her.

In Fr Fitzpatrick she had found that special peace that she had sought for a very long time. She had told Ted if she had another chance to live life again it would be very different - but she hadn't. I pray, God, that Ted never, ever feels that he did anything wrong in his dealings with Rose. In fact, I believe that this good man was sent to her and that they will meet up again (in a place where man does not lay down the rules and regulations) and that true peace will be truly theirs.

The time was fast approaching for us to say goodbye to Ted. This man has claimed a place in my heart and I am surprised to find that he has also touched Sally, because she had tears in her eyes as we left him. I hope I didn't hurt him by my coming. We had to go to Kath's for our breakfast and to say our goodbyes for the present. I found this more difficult than I thought I would. Kath was, as usual, very nervy, but at least she said she had slept well last night. I phoned John and he came up to Kath's. He had slept in this morning, then went to get me directions from Filey to Plymouth. While he was away, I had the following conversation with Kath:

'Johnny,' she said, 'I don't want to take you away from anyone, but yesterday, as you talked of Nuala, Marian and Kevin, I felt so hurt because you were speaking of them with such love.'

I explained that she couldn't - and indeed, wouldn't - take me away from anyone, but she could, in time, claim her place within my heart as they have.

I told her I had struggled with this question myself for a long time until I realised how big a heart my God has given me. The time had come for us to part and I talked to her of all of the feelings of insecurity that go with our stories, but that we must rise above it all by remembering who we are. I told her I was first and foremost (just as we all are) a child of God, born of Rose Bridget Kelly, first son of Mary (McCourt) and Eddie Mc Callion, husband of Sally Quigley, father of Edward, Stephen, Emmet, Catherine and Mary, brother of Nuala, Kevin and Marian, grandfather of Marie, Caoimhe, Matthew, Conor and Kevin, and (hopefully) friend of many.

So with this in mind, how can I feel insecure? I assured her, and then John, that this wasn't the end, but rather the beginning of our lives together. Kath cried and I was in control. John turned away and I called him back and saw the tears in his eyes. This man that I had met less than eighteen hours ago was crying because I was going, and so then my tears came. We hugged and then we parted, to meet again, I am sure. Who knows where and who knows when? God does.

And So, To Home

Monday, August 26th

Back home and back to work to live once more in the real world, with all that it holds for me and mine. I still have a few loose ends to tie up. I must get a copy of her marriage certificate and death certificate and carry out a trace of the children of Rose Bridget Kelly so that I can rest in peace in the knowledge that I have left no stone unturned.

I have to see Sr Bernadine and Fr Frank to fill them in on all that has happened since we last met. At the moment, I am feeling so drained and also a little bit disappointed - for myself.

I still haven't met anyone who can say, 'she told me of you, Johnny, and this is what happened'.

I still haven't been able to tell the two people who are most central to all of this about my search and findings over the past few months and I haven't been able to tell them that, without their love and care, I wouldn't have been able to cope with, or even accept, all that has unfolded about my past.

How I would love the opportunity to tell Mammy and Daddy. Please God, only this much do I ask today.

I spoke to Sr Bernadine; the words on the scroll that I brought back to her have a special meaning for her. It never fails to amaze me how God works, despite us.

Thank you, Sister, for everything. We will complete the journey at a later date.

The scroll I refer to was one I picked up while on holiday in England which started, *I went to the man at the gate of the year and said 'give me a light to show me the way', and he said 'put your hand in the hand of God and that will be better to you than any light'.*

I posted one to Sr Bernadine and one to Fr Frank. Why post them? Don't ask me... ask God.

* * * * *

Wednesday, August 28th

I went to Draperstown. As I drove over the mountain road from Feeny, I surveyed the beautiful valleys and hills that spread out before me, and as I inhaled the beauty of this place a sudden sadness filled my heart and my eyes misted over with tears. For, as I looked around me, I was reminded of a thought I'd had as I came towards Draperstown that first Monday, back at the beginning of my quest: *When I get all the pieces of this jigsaw in place, I may have to walk away from it all.*

Well, now they are in place and, for whatever reasons, the things those in Draperstown have decided to withhold from me (be it information or recognition) are never going to be mine: they have locked it all away in the vaults of their minds. I have decided this is the last time I would come here on this mission. Fr Frank is moving, too.

The Bishop has moved him to a new parish so we will be able to meet again.

This had been a worry of mine: how could I come to him in Draperstown without feeling cheated by those around and about? The scroll had arrived with him on the day the Bishop had sent for him; on a day he would need to be reminded of how special he was in God's eyes and how he needed to put his hand in the hand of the man at the gate of the year and how he needed to trust in Him. There again, I was thinking the message was only for me. Some God we have; if only we would let him run the full show.

*****

Monday, September 2nd

I am in pieces; in turmoil. Why do I feel like this? Why should I feel as I do? I don't know (well, you know what I mean). So much good in my life, so why am I letting this negativity take control of me? I feel like returning to Draperstown to claim all that is mine by right.

The truth from them is all I want. What happened to drive my Wild Irish Rose away from there, and did she tell them of me? I still, despite everything, believe they have known of my existence all along.

I feel so angry within; this prayerful and spiritual man is so hurt deep within.

Why haven't I found someone who knows of my being part of this story? It's not a lot to ask, is it?

To my family, I say please bear with me a little while longer; the moods are mine and I am very aware of them at this time. I am doing my best to overcome them, but, believe me, it isn't easy. I know all that you do for me and mean to me, but this void is hard to take and even harder to deal with at this time.

*****

Tuesday, September 3rd

Thank God for friends. Today has been awful, my mind has been looping the loop and I am getting more upset by the minute. Luckily,

I know that I can call on Johnnie White and be received as I am; warts and all.

I am so afraid that I make Sally and the wains feel that they and their love are not enough for me at this time.

This is about a lot more than that. This is about my very essence.

I go with him to the mountain of my God - An Grianán - and there I pour out a lot of the deep-down hurt, anger, fears and questions.

The child within, in a strange way, makes an appearance. Someday, Lord, maybe I will take the chance and set him totally free, to express himself... he has been suppressed for too long.

* * * * *

Wednesday, September 4th

Today, while still mulling over in my mind why someone from her time wouldn't acknowledge me or tell me why she may not have felt free to tell anyone of me, a thought struck me out of the blue: *What was your original mission? To tell Rose Kelly that all was OK, no matter what the reasons.*

You have lost sight of that, you have no control of it, so forget it; leave it alone. Peace that can only be given to me by God is mine, and I thank Him for that.

* * * * *

Wednesday, September 11th

I haven't got near the book since before the pilgrimage walk to Knock, simply because I was so drained and my zest had run very low. I am now beginning to feel better, and I will, I feel, return shortly to it. Again; unfinished business. It is good to be back home and it is good to be with the young people of the Holy Family youth support group. This is where I find love; this is where I find God.

* * * * *

Monday, September 30th

I met a lady today (her name is Rose) who shared a part of her story with me and finished by saying that she had come to the conclusion that something won't be answered until we get to the other side - and possibly then, it won't matter. When I said that recently I had made a journey into my own background and that I had come to the same conclusion, she then startled me with what she said next: 'Johnny, I have something I have wanted to say to you for a long time: I met you before you became Johnny McCallion; before you were adopted.'

She was around six or seven years old and a patient in the old eye, ear and throat hospital, on the Northland Road in Derry, and one morning she saw a nurse dressing this beautiful baby boy who was ten months old, or thereabout. She described the outfit as being a khaki colour and how the nurse laughed as she talked and dressed this baby. She told her he was going to the home (she wasn't sure if the nurse said Nazareth House or Termonbacca; both were local homes for children) and how shocked she was when the nurse told her this.

'He can't be,' said the seven-year-old girl.

'But he is,' the nurse replied. 'That is where he came from.'

And away the baby went. A while later, after she had returned to her own home in Lecky Road, she saw the child again. 'Johnny, you were with your daddy and I was the only child in the area who knew where you came from. Your daddy was so proud.'

My God never fails to surprise me. Here again, He supplied the answer to what seemed to be the unanswerable. Remember Sr Bernadine saying, 'but you shouldn't have been here' (in the Nazareth House in

Bishop Street)? Presumably, I was just passing through there on my way back to Fahan from the hospital. Or was I?

* * * * *

Monday, October 7th

The agitation of the weekend continues and I don't know what is going on again. I feel so disturbed, disrupted and uneasy. Something is stirring me up again but I don't know what it is.

Rose Kelly, in a strange way, came between Sally and me over the weekend when Sally expressed her concerns about what this quest was doing to me.

So clearly I hear her fears for both me and her in all of this. I took myself off to An Grianán on Saturday for a few hours and sat alone with my God and my thoughts.

I spent this evening with Johnnie White and we discussed many things in connection with it all: the implications of what I had uncovered over the past few months for me and all who are involved, whether by choice or not. I am sure that, in some way, it has been a help; time will tell.

* * * * *

Tuesday, October 8th

I awoke with the thought that the time has come to let go of Rose Kelly. I have been struggling with myself for the past while. I am glad that I now know why. I always said that I would know when the time was right... and it is now. The world that I know has told me all that it is going to tell me of her for now - unless my God tells me differently.

To those who have made this journey possible for me, I say thanks

155

- in particular to those of you who are not mentioned by name; you are part of my heart and no one can ever change that. The book is nearing completion and that will be another bit of the letting go process. I will have the Mass of thanksgiving for Rose Kelly to show my gratitude for her one gift to me and mine: the gift of life. Need I say more?

* * * * *

Author's note:

The above is the last entry of my diary.

Aftermath

May, 1997. One year had passed since I'd first gone to Draperstown. So what had happened with the passing of time, and where was I now with it all? Firstly, for months after my quest ended my mood swings still happened; maybe not with the frequency or intensity of before, but happen they did. Easter of '97 was a particularly bad time for me, to such an extent that I took Sally to meet Fr Frank so that we could go over the situation and come to an agreed plan on how to deal with what was happening.

By this time, Kath had provided me with the address of a lady in Belfast who appeared to have been a friend of Rose Kelly's in the 1940s and '50s. I had checked out the address and found that people with that name still lived there but I hadn't taken it any further. Father expressed surprise at this, saying this wasn't like the Johnny McCallion he'd met the year before in Draperstown:

'You wouldn't have hesitated in finding out the answer.'

I remember saying that this woman (if she was alive) might give me the answer that I didn't want to hear: that Rose didn't want me and never spoke of me. For that reason, the decision was made that it was time I went for some counselling. Some names were put on the table.

They would have to be damn good, otherwise I would simply dance rings around them and they wouldn't know which mask I was wearing.

We finally agreed on a certain person. I was happy enough. I was to make an appointment for as soon as possible. This I did, but the person I was looking for would not be available for some time; I was asked if I would speak to their partner? I agreed to do so, but the moment I put the phone down I knew it was the wrong decision - don't ask me why; just my gut feeling. I cancelled the appointment the next day, making some excuse. I decided to take my time. A few other names of noted counsellors came into my mind but they went as fast as they came.

The children had booked us into a hotel in Donegal for a weekend in early May, and I decided that no one was going to take away from this time with Sally; neither God nor Rose Kelly. In fact, someone asked me to pray for a particular intention, and I said I would - after the weekend. We laughed about it. So, on holiday from everyone we went. We had a lovely time, and on the Sunday, rather than going straight home after breakfast, we decided to head over to Dunfanaghy and go to Mass en route. I should have known better; I may have decided to take time away from God, but He never stops watching over me.

Anyway, into the chapel in Letterkenny we went, and as I lifted the leaflet to ponder over that day's readings I was left with tears in my eyes as I read that day's Gospel, which was 1 John 3:1: *Think of the love the Father has lavished on you by allowing you to be called God's children.*

And then, the line which really hit home (and which I am sure I had seen and heard many times before): *The reason the world does not know us is that it did not know him.*

It wasn't *me* they were rejecting; it was the God who created me.

Now I knew who my counsellor should be: the only one I couldn't dance around. The only one who would know which mask I was wearing; even better than I did myself. The only one before whom I stand naked as He looks into my very being... my Lord and my God.

Sally looked over at me and asked me what was wrong, for she had seen the tears in my eyes. 'Nothing,' was my reply. 'Everything is alright.' From then, the moods became less frequent.

They did happen now and again (I can be quite intolerant of certain situations) but slowly and surely, things were returning to normal. Funnily enough (but not surprisingly), I stopped doing as much writing. Instead, the writings took on the form of reflections or songs which seemed to come from nowhere, though I knew exactly where; it was my Counsellor at work.

Strangely, though, around the end of September '97, a thought came at me which had all the hallmarks of previous promptings from days gone by: if Father's contact had told anyone within the family circle about me, would it have been Tessie Moran, Rose's eldest sister? I knew I had to do something about it, but what? That was the question.

My work took me to Draperstown on occasion, but not so much to Desertmartin, where Tessie lived. But that wasn't a problem. We had a fella who used to cover that area who now ran a garage in Swatragh. So that's where I went. I chatted with him about his family and mine and other things of common interest to us both. Just as I was leaving, I asked him for some directions to several addresses, and in the middle of them I threw in the Morans of Desertmartin. 'That's his garage on your left, on the main road, from Tobermore to Desertmartin,' he said. 'And the home house, where his mother lives, is straight across the road.' Bingo! I had found Tessie. Now I had to devise a plan of approach ('attack' would be the wrong word). How will I get around this? I decided I would go in, give him my business card and watch his face for any reactions to the name. But I drove past just as he was locking up (probably for lunch) so I left it.

A few days later, I was in the area again on business and this time in I went. I handed him my card, by the way that I was looking to see if he was interested in buying oil from us. He looked at my card but gave no reaction. Now it was time for action. I asked him if he knew Rose Kelly. In fact, I asked, 'is she your mother's sister?' He said she was. I then explained that I had tried to approach the family, using Fr Frank as an intermediary, without any success. I had even driven along the road towards their home but had what I could only explain as a panic attack as the road narrowed. I couldn't breathe and I had to do a three-point turn and get off that road as fast as I could.

Then I told John (that was his name) that I wondered if his mother had been told of my coming to the area last year. I also explained that I knew his mother lived across the road and that if I wasn't a caring person, I could have gone straight to her. But I am a caring person and, having a mother of my own, I wouldn't want anyone to hurt her. He asked me if I was the postman (he was referring to Jimmy).

'No,' was my reply. 'I am the one that nobody knows of - or that will admit to knowing of.'

It was October 8th, the first anniversary of his father's death, John said; he wouldn't want to upset her today. This I could fully understand. We talked about many things that day and I agreed to call later to see how he'd gotten on with her. So once again to home, but this time I wasn't as burdened down as I had been before. I felt that this time I would get answers - one way or the other. John spoke of his brother, who lived at home with his mother, and his sister, who cared for her. He told me the family were known by the nickname the 'Hudie Kellys'. About ten days later, I called with him again, and by this time he had spoken to his brother Larry and sister Margaret about it all... but not his mother. They simply didn't know how to bring the matter up with her.

I had said on that first day that I needed to know if she had been told last year of the inquiries I made in Draperstown, and if so, had she decided for herself that she didn't want to meet me? This was the core of my mission in Desertmartin. As we talked, John's brother arrived and we chatted about all that had happened.

The more we talked, the more I realised that Father Frank's contact was not the right avenue of approach. But, as I said to Fr Frank later, one wrong move out of so many good ones wasn't so bad. Just think of the people on journeys like mine who, time after time over a period of months and years, have been given wrong information, or couldn't make headway because every road seemed to lead to a dead end. *I have been more than lucky,* was my summing up of the whole situation.

John and Larry both felt that their sister Margaret was the one who could broach the subject best with their mother. They asked me for a little more time. *What's another week or two?* I thought. I could wait. During my conversation with Larry, we were standing opposite their home, in full view of the living room window, and I was aware of a lady sitting at the window. Was this her? *It must be,* I concluded.

The following Saturday afternoon, Sally and I returned early from a break away because I had taken a very bad cold and she'd said I'd be more comfortable in my own bed. Ten or fifteen minutes after we got in, the phone rang. It was Larry, asking where I had been, adding that he had been looking for me since lunchtime. Margaret had been at home alone with her mother that morning when Tessie started looking at old photos and talking about her family. I wondered then had she seen me that day and had I triggered anything within her? I didn't ask; I just wondered. This was the opportunity Margaret had been waiting for. When she came to a photo of Rose, she told her mother about me. Then she asked if anyone had recently told her about me; she said she hadn't heard anything. *Once again,* I thought, *my gut feeling was right.* I wondered was this the gift of discernment - knowing something through the power of the Spirit - at work. How often during my life had this feeling turned out to be right, and in a variety of situations?

Tessie said she would like to meet me. No longer ruled by the impetuosity of my earlier days, I arranged to meet her, not the next week but the following one. Sure hadn't I the flu on me and I had to get over that first? I should have known better; by the end of the next week, I was on edge again. My emotions were running riot and, yet again, time wasn't going fast enough.

Finally, the appointed day and time arrived. I left the house well before I had to; I needed time and space to prepare and gather myself and put on whatever mask I needed to wear that night. I arrived at their home and Larry came out to meet me. We walked into the house and there, at last, stood before me this lady who, if my calculations were right, was in her early eighties. She was not in the least as I had imagined her; I wonder how she felt in my presence. After the initial awkwardness, we settled down and relaxed into each other's company and I filled her in about my journey and my reason for it all. I told her of Mammy and Daddy, Sally and the gang and all the people who had made my life special because of the love they had shown me.

I had taken a selection of my reflections which I gave to her so that she could read them in her own time, and had included an explanation of my reasons for writing them. We talked that night of many things, but several times I noticed tears come to Tessie's eyes as we touched on things relating to Rose, in particular. I sensed her pain as she tried to answer questions (which I knew only Rose could) that weren't hers to answer. I tried to explain that I didn't expect her to be able to give me those answers; that was Rose's right, and when we met up in the next world it wouldn't matter. Then we started talking about her family.

They were surprised to learn how much I had discovered about them and we laughed as I told them I probably knew more about the Kellys than they did themselves. I said the dead revealed themselves to me while the living seemed to hide from me. Margaret was also there and I could see a similarity between her and Kath; the same sort of build and height and features.

Tessie had photos of her family, past and present, to show me. I was amazed when she produced a photo of one of her own sons when he was young and I could see the similarity between myself and him at that stage. She had photos of him later on but I couldn't see it then. Lastly, she produced a photo that she said she wanted me to take: it was from seventy-odd years earlier and was of her mother and father, older brother John (who had died following an asthma attack, of all things, when he was just 29 years old), herself and the twins; Rose and May.

Finally, I was able to put faces to the names I had seen on the grave in the old Keenaght cemetery in Desertmartin. It was a strange feeling but somehow seemed appropriate that the dead should also be revealed in this earthly way at last. I had often wondered who, if any of us, resembled Rose Kelly. The question was now answered; and I must say, the revelation was startling. There was no likeness of her in my own children, but from that photo, I could see she had come out in our granddaughter, Caoimhe. Everyone thought she was her mother's image; but not anymore - even the shape of her hair, you would have thought it had been styled by the exact same hairdresser that had done Rose's.

Another question has been answered, I thought. *Yet more of the jigsaw is in place.*

But again, the elusive piece was missing: Rose hadn't told Tessie of me.

During this time, I had to live in the real world, with all its joys, trials, and tribulations. Mammy, as usual, was giving so much of herself and doing what she did best: caring for others, even though she herself was now 85 years old. My aunt Kath wasn't well (she had been diagnosed with Alzheimer's) and this was causing Mammy great concern. I watched the tears come to her eyes as she spoke of her. I had gone with her to the hospital and seen the pain in her eyes as we left Kath behind us and I heard the agony in her voice as she tried to reason why Kath had this terrible, cruel disease. I tried to say that we must look at the quality of life a person has before we ask God to extend that life, but I think this horrified her. But really, what I was trying to say is that the time had come when we must let go and let God sort it out. Not easy to do, but as I looked at Kath and Daddy, I worried for Mammy and what their illnesses were doing to her.

Daddy's health was still a great cause for concern for us all. The way I saw it, he was fading away, and at times I would look at his quality of life and wonder, *why?* It was at such times that I realised what I wanted was the man of my yonder years. One day, I was standing at the front of the altar before I took Communion to the sick; this was the time when I would normally pray for Rose. But this particular week was different, for some reason. This time I prayed to her, asking her to go to God on my behalf and ask Him to return the man of my yonder years. The incident inspired me to write the following song:

The Man of My Yonder Years

As I look at you now, I just wonder how,
Yonder years have come and gone,
When I was so young and you so strong,
Now I see what our journey has done.

For the head once held proud, is now bent and bowed,
With years of trial and pain,
And the hands once so hard, no longer are gnarled,
They won't work for a living again.

As I look at you now, with a heart that's in two,
I wipe away all my tears,
Asking what can I do to bring back the you,
The man of my yonder years.

But you I must free so all this can be,
Just as you once let go of me,
Then I was so young in the midst of life's fun,
That I missed out on our yonder years.

Our roles they have changed though our hearts are the same,
As the boy leads the man now it's true,
Soon the time will come and then we'll be one,
And look back on our yonder years.

For I know in my heart someday we will part,
Somewhere down along this road,
Don't go before I say that I love you today,
Just as I did in our yonder years.

Don't go before I say that I love you today,
Just as I did in our yonder years.

My God had answered many prayers and I was not going to limit Him by saying, 'he won't answer this one'. I knew, from experience, it would be in His way and in His time.

Deepest Sorrow

By June 1998, Daddy's health had failed to such an extent that he and Mammy had to come and live with us. She was no longer able to tend him on her own. This was to turn out to be a very special time for us all. I only thought I knew the depth of our love for each other; what happened over the next five weeks was to prove that beyond all doubt. Though he could walk from place to place around the house, Daddy was finding everything more difficult, day by day. Firstly, he had to be helped to the bathroom, then he had to be shaved and helped in many ways. He must have found all this very embarrassing, to say the least. He was a very private man.

I remember the first time I had to shave him. My hand was shaking, more so than usual. (Someone in the Kelly family, I had discovered during the course of my research, suffered from a tremor. Was this a legacy from my past?) He must have been afraid that I would cut his throat, and I couldn't blame him. I was so scared of hurting him in any way. As time went by, I got the courage not to be so tentative and found I was managing not too badly. Or was I?

I remember saying to him one day: 'Daddy, I was thinking of giving up my job and opening a barber's shop specialising in shaves.'

He told me to stick to what I was good at! Some boost to my confidence. I then joked that I was going ahead with the idea and calling the place 'Eddie Wouldn't Let Me Shave Him' - as you see, we laughed a lot in our family.

His health continued to go downhill and it was hard to watch Mammy watch him deteriorate; she was blocking out the long-term prognosis.

But though he was getting progressively worse, he was alert to everything and I remember going to the bathroom with him on one occasion and he was very embarrassed (so much so that he had tears in his eyes) and I said, 'Daddy, there is nothing that I am doing for you that you haven't already done for me'. We finished what we were doing and as I took him by the arm to help him out to the sitting room, he stopped, put his arms around my neck, pulled me close to him and said, 'I suppose that is love, Johnny'. Whose eyes were the tears in now?

Kevin was in and out of the house every day. Nuala and Marian were always phoning and, in their own ways, were always there to help in whatever way they could. Mary, in my eyes, matured beyond her years from the wain that was always cared for, especially by Mammy and Daddy, to become the carer. Her gentleness was limitless and her love unconditional. Again, the rock upon which I am built - Sally - was there at every corner; helping, loving and understanding, in the right order, as the situation called for.

Mammy was hoping, before Marian came in early July, that Daddy's health would improve enough to allow them to go back to their own house so she could stay with them there, but that wasn't to be; Daddy wasn't getting any better. Marian came to stay with us instead, and on July 6th he was admitted to hospital with what the doctor thought was a kidney or urine infection. But he wasn't to know what was happening inside of Daddy's body. The hospital staff were shocked when a routine chest x-ray showed there had been a major perforation somewhere between the stomach and the bowel area, but because of the general condition of Daddy's health an operation to locate the problem and sort it was out of the question.

By 7.30pm on Tuesday, July 7th, we had been told that he was on borrowed time. The consultant, Mr Gilliland, was reluctant to put a time on it, but then I asked him the question another way: 'When do you expect to do your rounds and not see Daddy here?'

He looked at me and said: 'If he is still here in a week's time, he will be doing well'.

He was very gentle with Mammy and told her that he would make sure Daddy was as comfortable as possible, assuring her he would have no pain at all. She wanted to take him home but that wasn't possible, was what he said. It was time to gather the clan; the chips were down and we could draw strength from each other. The phone calls weren't easy to make.

At least Marian was already here, so that was one less call to make. Day by day, Daddy deteriorated. Nuala, Emmet and Catherine arrived; we were family and clan again. My relationship with Daddy entered a new phase: it is easy to pray with and for others openly, but I know I tend to hold back in the presence of my own - but this situation was different. I couldn't pray for healing for Daddy but I prayed that God would be gentle with him and Mammy at this time.

Why not healing? I can almost hear you ask. Well, some years before, I had prayed for healing for Daddy as he lay in the coronary care unit. And so, this time, God reminded me of my earlier insight into all that lies ahead for us in His Heavenly Kingdom and I knew then that I didn't have the right to hold this great man, my earthly father, back from his eternal reward. I then prayed, for the first time ever in my life, *Thy will be done.* There is, indeed, a far more important healing than that of the body: the healing of the soul. That is the big gift from God.

Psalm 23 became central to our prayer time together over the next few days. Firstly, we prayed together and then, as his voice failed, I prayed for both of us aloud. On Sunday, July 12th, I was praying with Daddy after Kevin and Marian had gone home to get some sleep - they had sat up all night with him, as we had been doing since Wednesday because of the worsening situation. When we had finished praying, I was sitting holding his hand and I asked him, 'Daddy, what has this life been all about?'. He looked at me. He didn't speak (he couldn't), but somehow we communicated in spirit, or in thought, the following conversation:

Daddy: *We have been painting a picture of love.*

Me: *A picture of love? You'll have to explain that one to me a bit more, Daddy; I don't understand.*

Daddy: *In a place and time now long forgotten, God called us all to a meeting, and the minutes of that meeting are recorded in the book of life, and the following is a copy of that record:*

Let's paint a picture of love, they did hear their God say,
Let's paint a picture of love, to help you on your way,
We will start at the very beginning, and add colours as we go,
And each day of the story will tell of times from long ago.

We'll take a loving couple, give them four children from above,
Each will bring their colours to paint this picture of love,
They will come from different places, and come at various times,
Each bringing their bits and pieces, to complete this work divine.
At times throughout this journey, they will forget what God did say,
For they are only human and will try it their own way,
But God will always remind them with a gentle nudge from above,
That the main point of this journey was to paint a picture of love.

There will be times for joy and sorrow, times for laughter and pain,
But they will paint this picture and close they will remain,
And when they finish this mission and gather up above,
Then they will hear their God say,

'Sure it's a beautiful picture of love'

Here, in the silence of our hearts, came the answers to all my questions. Here, in this hospital room, I came face to face with my past. Over the years, I had heard people say that we should give our guardian angel a name. Once again, I was blind, but now I could see. In my early years, God provided me with two angels: one called Eddie and the other called Mary. My Mammy and Daddy. In later years, He added another: Sally.

Talking of Mammy, at one stage on the following day (Monday 13th), she and I were on our own with Daddy, who was sleeping, when she said to me, 'Johnny, you shouldn't be going through this. If we hadn't taken you all, you may have done better for yourselves'.

'What are you on about now?' I asked.

Her reply astounded me: 'Well, you might have got someone with more money and bigger houses who could have given you more than we have.'

'I suppose you're right,' I replied, 'but then, maybe in all of that, there may have been no love. I'll settle anytime for the love that we have received from both of you. Did it ever strike you that if you hadn't come along when you did, we wouldn't have known that love?'

If only she knew.

Many things happened during this special time whose value no money or earthly possessions could ever match, never mind surpass. They were priceless personal memories of a man and woman sent to us by God to guide us on our ways. On Tuesday, July 14th, at 7.50pm, Daddy died. The earthly chain was broken, the Eternal one begun.

'Your father was a special man,' someone said to me at my Daddy's wake as he shook my hand.

I asked him, 'what do you mean, special?', and this was his reply:

'He mixed with the highest and walked with the lowest and was comfortable with them all.' Need I say more? We were determined to celebrate his life, and I pray that we did him proud during this time.

How to care for Mammy was now the major focus in our lives. We had experienced the emotional turmoil, insecurity and loss (all that is tied up in the grieving process) of one who had gone from all our lives, but none of us could begin to imagine how she felt. They had been married for 58 years - a lifetime together.

I remember going home one day earlier that year and being aware that something was wrong because Mammy had gone straight into the kitchen when I came in and Daddy seemed strange, for some reason, so I asked what was wrong.

'Your mother will tell you when she comes in' he said. In she came. 'What's up with you two?", I asked.

Eventually, she told me that, before I had come in, they had been discussing the fact that if one of them was to die, the other would not be around much longer because they couldn't live without each other. I told them that they had certainly fulfilled any promise or commitment made to us and that if that was how it was to be, then OK.

Mammy brought this very same subject up to me one day in October when I called in to see how she was. She went home the night Daddy died and stayed by herself after the funeral - her choice of how she was to carry on.

She said: 'I don't think I have too long to go, but I must know that it is OK to go, so you must tell me if it is.'

I am sure my reply stunned her, because a month before, I had written the following reflection which already held the answer:

He Walked By Her Side

He walked by her side, ever holding her hand,
And promised he'd never let go,
But life it is full of its own twists and turns,
There were things that he couldn't know.

Now he's gone from her world, let go of her hand,

She knows it's now all in the past,
To this heart which is broken, she holds her wedding band,
'What can I do now?' she asks.

She hears many voices, all filled with love,
But the one that she wants now is stilled,
They want to protect her from this pain that is hers,
But the void in her life can't be filled.

In the midst of the crowd, she sits all alone,
The one she loves now has gone,
What has happened their dreams? What's happened their hopes,
Which they shared this whole life long?

Now she waits on her time, for that was their plan,
Made not very long before,
So when it comes round, he'll take her by the hand,
And they'll walk as in years of yore.

Of course, I told her it was alright to go, whenever the time was right.
No conditions; just unconditional love was all I could give her now.

The God Of Surprises

I remember Sr Bernadine saying once, 'Johnny, God can move mountains'. Well, he certainly can, because in late 1998, the door that was once closed to me was opened: I met Rose Kelly's twin sister, May. How did this come about? Once again, the Spirit of God was at work in my life, for on October 1st, I had left Dungiven on my way to Maghera, via the Glenshane Pass, only to find myself diverting onto the road to Draperstown.

What's happening now? I asked myself, but, in my heart, I knew from experience the agitation from days of yore was back. I was very aware of God's presence at that time. *What has happened since you first came here in May 1996?*

Then, for some reason, those who had died became the focus of my thoughts. It was then that I was challenged (as only God can) with the following thought: *Time is getting short and there is one door still to be opened: it may well be your greatest fear, but face it you must.*

Having prayed to God and my Daddy for guidance, I came into Draperstown and, after buying some flowers, headed up the road to her home, which was just a few miles beyond Draperstown. The last time (in fact, the only other time) I had travelled this way, I thought I was suffocating, and, in a panic, turned the car and headed back to Draperstown; but not on this occasion.

Fr Frank may have been using the wrong key to try and unlock this door that I need to get through, was the thought that struck me.

It was then that I realised that I maybe knew how to find the location of the other three keys. I had an idea that the two houses were close to each other, so when I had travelled the full length of the road I turned into a shared driveway, taking the one which I had decided must be the right one. I drove the car into the yard and a lady came out to speak to me. I gave my name to her and she didn't react. For a moment, I thought I had come to the wrong place. But when I mentioned Rose Kelly, the penny dropped. Her name was Josie; she was May's daughter. I explained that I wasn't there to cause hurt to anyone but said I was glad I had met her so that she could make up her own mind regarding what I was about. She then invited me into her home and one of the first things she said was, 'why didn't you do this twenty or thirty years ago?' I chose to leave that one until later, for I sensed I needed this lady on my side if I was to make any progress at all.

We talked for over an hour and I filled her in on what I had discovered along the way. At one point, she remarked that she felt she should take me to meet her mother but she was worried that the shock would upset her. This lady loves her mother, I thought. She wants to protect her. I didn't blame her for that; I would do the same for Mammy. Then I pointed out that her mother was central to my journey. She was as near as I could get to Rose in human form. I did say that, even if she decided to take me to mother there and then, I would not be going. I wanted her to take her time and ponder all that I had told her, and then to phone me with her mother's answer, in her own time.

As I left, Josie asked me why I hadn't gone straight to her mother's house next door. I would have, I said, if she had come out to meet me. But she didn't, and I believe that I was meant to meet her instead. Then I answered her earlier question of why not twenty or thirty years ago, saying the same to her as I did to Fr Frank:

'I don't know if I could have accepted all that has been revealed in the same way back then as I have now.'

Later that month, Josie phoned me to say her mother was happy to talk, so I arranged to go up and see her the following Monday. May was a nice woman. I didn't hear anything from her that I didn't already know - I may even have filled in the gaps for her. But though she had no big revelations for me, there was no denial of me by her, either, which is all I really wanted. Ironically, the meeting took place on November 2nd - All Souls' Day. I know that Daddy, in his way, was at my side for it, as indeed Rose must have been as well.

The Child Reflects

So, where did I sit with everything that had happened over the last few years? Well, just read the reflection below, which I wrote in early 1999. Hopefully, it will become clear to you how and why I was able to feel so secure. And able, finally, to put Rose Kelly to rest...

The Child Reflects

Time for reflection. What, and who, has this journey been all about, and where do I go from here? The thought that comes strongest to me at this time is that the 'man' part of me never has had a problem with all that has happened since I was born; sure I have said it often enough. I am who I am because that is the way my God planned it. But what about the child deep within me? I pray that I can set him free - or maybe even free him long enough to do this reflection so that he may be heard at last. So it's over to you, kid: be gentle with me, please. I am so fragile and you must take it from here.

I am the child from the womb; the child from long, long ago. I am the child no one knows of, the child the world said wouldn't know any better, 'what he doesn't have he'll never miss'. I am the child that couldn't, or wouldn't, feel any sense of rejection - at least, that is what was said (or thought) by those who had a say in deciding that I should go as I did, at birth. The world would tell you, 'sure isn't he OK now? Hasn't he got a good - no, in fact, a great - home, and a mother and father who genuinely love him? Isn't he part of a very secure and loving family, with a brother and two sisters? Isn't he happily married with a wife and children of his own, all of whom love him deeply, and hasn't another generation started to come along, and doesn't he love each one of them with a love beyond all understanding?'

The answer to all these questions is 'yes'. But there is a gap in all this, and it is this time - the time before all those good things happened to me - that concerns me, so it is this that I want to talk about. I wonder if I was a welcome visitor in my birth mother's womb. What about the day of my birth; was there any rejoicing then, or was it all resentment? Had things been said by someone, while I was the child in the womb, that had led to my going? What were her feelings on the day of separation? And when was that day? They say a child will never know, but I can only wonder if that was true. Why did I have to go? What kind of life did I have until I came to Mammy and Daddy, to be their own?

Am I the child who was never fed at the breast? Am I the child who never knew natural bonding? Am I the child who doesn't know who cuddled him or soothed him when he cried? Am I the child who was never held in her arms, the child she never kissed or said she loved? Did she ever acknowledge me as hers, or nurse me on her knee and sing me to sleep? Am I the child of unfulfilled or broken dreams?

I wonder who watched this child as he made his way out into the world, as he discovered his toes, his feet, his nose, ears, mouth and eyes. Who held his hand as he learned to walk? Who heard his first word? Who reached out to him as he took his first steps on his own? Who cared when he wasn't well? Who watched him play as a child? Who was it that found his first tooth, and, as the custom is today, bought him his first pair of shoes? Where was the stability in his life? In whose arms did he feel safe and secure and who told him to have no fear? It wasn't you, Rose Kelly. It wasn't you.

So what have I been feeling after all of this time and during this journey? I'll tell you now at last. I have been angered by the feelings of hurt and rejection that have been mine all these years. I have been questioning what the hell had been going on when Rose Kelly walked away. Draperstown saved their faces, the boy and the man got his mother, father, family and friends, but me: what did I get? Nothing! At times my rages would well up and I wanted to hit out, but at what, and who, I did not know. Frustration, rawness and brokenness: all are words that describe my feelings throughout this time. Isolation is another and I have no doubt there are many, many more. Peace certainly wasn't mine in any form, shape or fashion, but at last, I am moving towards that goal. I know my moods will swing to and fro for a while, but I have noticed that this is not happening as often as in the past. The Lord is healing me.

All these questions or statements may give the impression that I am not grateful for all that has happened in my life since then. Let there be no mistake: I, just like the man, would not change one iota of my life since then, but unlike the man, I cannot accept logically my life before that day. For I am only a child, with a child's need to be loved always; not just some of the time. I suppose my main query is, 'was I not loved? And if not, why not?'

I have, during this journey to Desertmartin and Draperstown, come to realise that some questions won't and can't be answered until we meet again in a later life in heaven, and then my Wild Irish Rose can have her say. That said, I have come to know her better throughout this time of the present, from the people I have met who knew her. I find it amazing that the dead from her townland revealed themselves to me while the living hid. I wonder, at times, who the living really are. I just wonder.

I thank God for His protection of us both, not just over the past few months but since this life journey began. The thing I find hardest to accept is the fact that she may not have told anyone of me. People have tried to reassure me that she didn't give me up easily, but I haven't met anyone who can tell me that for sure, simply because, up until this time, I haven't come across one person she told of me. Even Jimmy can trace directly back to her and her feelings for him. I can't, and, for me, this is the hardest part of all.

Now that I know the man has moved heaven and earth in his quest for answers on my behalf, I can be at peace. He certainly has had his share of pain and heartache, as well, during this journey. But, most of all, he has had a great depth and strength of faith. I pray that this faith never fails him.

I remember one day, in particular, when Fr Frank asked him if he was sorry that he hadn't started this search twenty years before and I was amazed by his answer. With hindsight, I now know he was right, for the child then could have dealt with and accepted all that had been recently revealed, but the man of then certainly couldn't have. In fact, I don't know what it would have done to him.

Finally, the man said that this journey was about releasing someone from a self-imposed prison. I have news for him: it was I who had to be freed, it was I who was crying in the darkness, it was I who was lost and wandering in the wilderness. It is I who am now found, now prepared to walk in peace with this God who has made the man and me one at last, in His love, and I live with the knowledge that anything that hasn't been revealed up until now will be in God's time. My thoughts have inspired the following song:

Little Children of Our God

Chorus: Little children, little children, little children of this world,
Little children, little children, little children of our God.

If we'd been given diamonds, if we'd been given pearls,

If we'd been given jewels, sure none could compare,
To the gifts our God has given to each and every one,
Who is part of this family centred in His Son.

To us He's given treasures, and none have been so rare,
He's shown us a way in which there's no despair,
He's given us a hope, a light that will not dim,
As we lead His little children on the road back home to Him.

For some it may be heavy, for others very light,
We must be centred in Him if we're to do it right,
It would be better for them to tie a rock around our necks,
Than to take one of His children down the road to hell and back.

Who are these little children, the children of His flock,
Who are the jewels in His crown which He won't let us rock?
There's you and then there's me and this whole world roundabout,
We are the children of our God, of this let's have no doubt.

This world has taught me many things, but God has taught me not to put my faith in mortal man; he will only let me down. Believe me, there is enough in that teaching to help me write another book. Someday, just maybe, I will.

PART THREE

LETTING IN THE LIGHT

There's More...

When I finished writing the reflection that brings part two of this book to an end, I felt I had finally found peace. And so I laid down my pen. For me, at that time, there was nothing more to write. Just like the child of the womb, the man of the world was at peace with himself, sure in the knowledge that, if I needed to know any more to help me along life's highway to Heaven, as I added my colours to this picture of love, then all would be revealed in God's time.

I had thought the story of my search for Rose, and how I finally found my peace with it all, was the only story I would ever write. If there was anything more to be told, maybe someone else (one of the children, for example) might decide to do that at a later date. But it turns out I wasn't quite done yet: in November 2014 I was moved to start writing again, fifteen years after I'd last put pen to paper. Why, Johnny? I hear you ask.

Well, the truth is, a lot happened in the subsequent years that even I could not have reckoned on; a lot that changed my way of thinking and a lot that changed my way of evaluating what was important to me in life and what wasn't. When I last put pen to paper in early 1999, the world was fast approaching a new era (or dawn) in its own ongoing story of evolution with the coming of the new millennium.

A time of great wonder and awe, of excitement and expectation, lay ahead of us. But it was mixed with a tangible feeling of apprehension as the prophets of doom and gloom had a field day with prophecy after prophecy of one impending disaster after another.

I suppose, somewhere in between these differing outlooks, lay the truth, as we have had many wonderful things that have taken place since then while, at the same time, we have witnessed the horrendous catastrophic events of 9/11 and all that has followed in its footsteps.

In the midst of all of this, the lives of ordinary folk like ourselves continued to unfold with twists and turns that none of us could have expected. If you haven't realised by now that the most important thing in my life is the well-being and welfare of my family, then let me reassure you - in no uncertain terms - that it is.

And that is why the remainder of this book is all about them.

A Close Call

I vividly recall the planning Sally and I did to make sure that as many of us who were able would spend New Year's Eve, 1999, together at our home. After all, it wasn't just the New Year but the new millennium. Only a handful of generations, since the time Jesus walked among us, had been able to celebrate this great milestone in the story of mankind.

If truth be told, 1999 was not the best of years for us as a family. We were all missing Daddy, each in our own way, while trying to care for Mammy, who had suffered the greatest loss of all of us. My own health suffered and I succumbed to deep-set pneumonia in early February which saw me off work for four months; I now believe that this happened because I didn't allow myself any space or time to grieve the massive loss of my Daddy. Our grandson also had some health issues this year, so maybe this shows why 1999 was a year that I, personally, was glad to say goodbye to.

Though she had retired from teaching in June '98, Sally had taken up a tutoring role working with people who hoped to become valued assistants in schools. It was becoming more obvious, as the year progressed, that Sally's own health wasn't as good as it should be, but, Sally being Sally, she battered on regardless. That's Sally: if any of us had even a drop of her commitment and dedication then the world would be a better place.

But we still wanted to plan something special, regardless. What a gift we had been given in being one of these families who has shared in this celebratory rite of passage from one millennium to the next. That was our driving force: we felt the privilege was all ours, as the elders of our family, to help guide the young (and not-so-young) of the Derry clan McCallion forward, into the unknown, just as pioneers had done, from age to age, before us. I wonder how many others thought or felt as we did back then.

That is the background to what was unfolding. It was a time of great hope and expectation (within our family, anyway) as we had found out in the September and October that the clan McCallion was about to be expanded by three new arrivals, if all went well, sometime between March and May of the year 2000. Edward and Clare, Stephen and Noreen and Catherine and Pat were the expectant parents who had so much to look forward to that coming year.

Those of our children and grandchildren who were able to be there gathered with us as we welcomed in the New Year; our world was complete and we were at peace. Everyone stayed over and we slept heads and toes, as they say. We breakfasted (or I should say 'brunched') together, relaxed and welcomed the year 2000, in its infancy, into our midst. As evening time approached, our children and grandchildren set off to their own homes and Sally and I settled down to a quiet evening to unwind. Mammy was due to come back from Kevin's in a few days. She spent Christmas with us and had then gone to Kevin's for a few days to catch up with them.

Mammy had come to stay with us permanently in the middle of 1999 as her health was starting to fail and Sally had said that we couldn't leave her on her own anymore. We'd asked Mammy if she would like to come to stay with us, reassuring her that the family home in Creggan would always be kept and that she could return to it if she ever wanted to. It was important that we helped her to maintain her independence for as long as possible. She agreed to this suggestion, albeit with a bit of regret and fear as to how her world was changing. She never did go back to live permanently in our family home but she did go and stay there for a few weeks, from time to time, whenever Nuala or Marian came over from England to be with her and to give us some respite.

Anyway, at around 11pm, I said to Sally that I was heading to bed as I was exhausted, and she said that she would come up later. I was asleep when Sally came into our bedroom and woke me up to say she had a terrible pain in her back. It felt like I'd been asleep for hours but it was only 11.30pm. I knew that Sally must be in a lot of pain as, unlike me, she never normally complained. We phoned the out-of-hours doctors. They gave her an urgent appointment and we went straight there. They thought that it may be gallstones or something like that, so they gave her some pain relief and we headed home. But, two hours later, we were back again; the pain had gotten worse. This time they said that she would have to go into hospital immediately, and by 4am on January 2nd, 2000, the nightmare had begun.

This was to turn out to be a life-changing experience for all of us as a family (not least for Sally herself) because, by the Friday, the diagnosis had changed dramatically from gallstones. Sally had been waiting for a slot to have an ultrasound carried out to confirm the preliminary diagnosis.

As the radiographer carried out the procedure on her right side, in the region of the gallbladder, she asked Sally where the pain was, to which Sally replied that it was all around her abdomen: front and back. So the radiographer went over to the left-hand side and took images of that area and said someone would come to see her with the results before she left for home.

I was over at the hospital later that evening and Edward and Clare had come over to join us. A young doctor came in and said that things were no clearer than before; an appointment would be sent out to her to come back later to the outpatients clinic. It really was quite confusing and worrying, because, to tell the truth, the doctor didn't seem to know what was happening. Sally said that I should go out for my tea with

Edward and Clare but I was too worried as to what was going on with her to even think of eating. I headed home and put on the kettle to have a cup of coffee. While the kettle was boiling, the phone rang. It was Sally. She said, 'Johnny, maybe you should come on over again, I have something to tell you'.

It was the most awful journey I have ever made; I knew Sally wouldn't ask me to come back just after I had left her without there being a good reason.

She met me in the corridor of the ward and said we needed to talk. A consultant, Mr Bateson, had come in to see her just after we had left for home and told her that the scan had shown that there was something on her left kidney. Sally asked if he was referring to cancer; he said he was and that the oncology consultant would be in to discuss the situation in the morning before she went home. We decided that we wouldn't tell the wains anything until after this meeting on Saturday so that we could at least protect them for one more night from whatever lay ahead.

I was over very early the next morning. The oncology consultant, Mr Lennon, came in just after 10am and confirmed that it was, indeed, cancer, and therefore the kidney would have to be removed. We asked if Sally could have any treatment other than surgery, such as chemo and the like, but that wasn't to be: kidney cancer, he said, was not responsive to chemotherapy so the only option was to remove the sickly kidney.

At home now, we had to face the wains and tell them what was wrong with Sally before they might hear a whisper from someone else. We phoned them and asked them to come up to see Mammy and to bring the grandchildren; Sally wanted to see them all as she had been missing them while she had been in hospital. Mary and Emmet were at home, anyway, and Edward and Stephen came up within half an hour; I honestly can't remember if they brought the children with them. The only one missing was Catherine as, with her living down in Cork, we had played things very low-key with her during Sally's week-long stay in hospital. It was obvious that they knew something was seriously wrong with Sally and I broke down when we started to talk. Luckily, Sally had the strength that deserted me and it was she who calmly told them what had come to pass the day before. Then she phoned Catherine, and, again, I honestly don't know where she got the strength to do it. But only Sally could do it - she carried all of us. The wains were devastated and I was at a total loss as to what to do next.

Sally had her operation on the first Tuesday in February. But about a week after her operation (by which time, Mr Lennon had told us when we'd first spoken to him, Sally would be on her way home to make a complete recovery), she told the nursing staff that she was in great pain and felt something was wrong. But they didn't listen to her; in fact, she was moved out of the side ward she had been in and onto the main ward. Within fifteen hours, we were facing another major crisis.

I got a phone call at around 5.30am advising me to come straight to the hospital as Sally was in quite a distressed state and very agitated. Since her operation, I had been in the hospital from around 6.30am each morning, as I couldn't settle myself if I wasn't there with her. When I arrived, the place was in turmoil. They had moved Sally back into a side ward again. Five or six doctors were gathered around her bed and all I could get from her was, 'Johnny, they wouldn't listen to me. I told them that I was in agony with a pain in my shoulder, but they said that they were busy with a new admission and left me there'.

I was to find out later what had really happened. Sally asked for them to phone me to come over to be with her if they were too busy to deal with her and they refused, saying something to the effect that this wasn't a single ward and she should phone me herself. Obviously, later, the penny dropped with them that Sally was indeed a very ill patient so the first thing they did was to make moves to cover their backs.

One of the doctors came to me and said that, while some were saying the pain was coming from this area and that area, he himself felt that it was referred pain and the most likely place it was coming from would be the wound site; the shoulder was a nerve ending spot for things to do with the abdomen area.

By this time, it was almost 7am and he said he had contacted Mr Lennon, who would be with us ASAP. True to his word, Mr Lennon arrived within fifteen minutes of that call, and, after seeing Sally, he spoke to me and said that he needed to get a scan carried out to help him find out what was going on. He then went on to say that the x-ray theatres didn't open until 9am and he would have to wait until then to find out how quickly the scan could be done. It was 8am at this point and the time seemed to go ever so slowly. Meanwhile, I realised that the situation was now a serious one and that I would need to alert the wains and anyone else who needed to know.

Nine o'clock came and nine o'clock went. Nurses were in and out; Sally's niece Lorraine came down from the ward she was nursing on and that made things a little easier. Nearer and nearer to 10 o'clock the time went, when suddenly everything on the monitoring machine went blank. Mr Lennon had been in just before that and had gone to find news about a time for the scan. I told the young nurse who was with us at this time that she should get someone who would know what to do. Mr Lennon rushed into the ward, took one look at the monitor and said to me he didn't have time to talk to me. He dragged Sally's bed out of the ward and towards the operating theatres, which were on the same floor as us and just across the corridor from the side ward that Sally was in. I was left standing in an empty ward, not knowing what to think other than I needed the wains with me. I had to know that they were OK. Just then, they started arriving; Stephen and Emmet came first. Mary was at teacher training college in Belfast having final meetings with her tutors before setting out on her first-year trainee placement (how Mary ever got through that time amazes me when I think of the pressure she was under) and Edward was somewhere in Fermanagh; his company was trying to contact him. Catherine had to come up from her home in Macroom in Cork.

Our daughters-in-law, Clare and Noreen, had arrived, and our Kevin was there as well. Sally's brothers, Tommy and Michael, and their wives Tillie and Eugena had arrived with members of their families to offer us support - and I am sure to be supported themselves in this hour of great need. A lot of our personal friends came to the hospital, as well, to support us. It was 1.30pm before Mr Lennon came back from the operating theatre to tell us that Sally was now in the recovery area and that she would be going to the intensive care unit. He said that, as she was quite ill, she had been very heavily sedated to give her body a chance to recover from the shock of a second invasive surgery within a week. The problem, he said, was that Sally's spleen had ruptured and that there was no option but to remove it.

It was a long day and night, to say the least, as we didn't know if she would have the strength to cope with all she had been through in the last seven days. One of Mary's tutors kindly brought her down from Belfast. Catherine had to fly from Cork to Birmingham, then on to Belfast, as that was the only connection she could get in the emergency. Her childhood friend, Seana, picked her up in Belfast and brought her straight to the hospital in Derry. The road conditions were awful that evening, as we'd had quite heavy snowfall in the North during the day. Edward didn't get home until later as the area he was in had a very bad phone signal and driving conditions were treacherous.

The following day, Mr Lennon told me that if Sally had been down in the scanning area of the hospital when the crisis struck, he and I wouldn't be having this conversation; he wouldn't have been able to do anything in time to save her. That is how close we came to losing Sally.

It was to be another three weeks before we got her home to continue with her recovery, which was to be a long-drawn-out affair. Sally had lost a good three or four stone in weight and, obviously, her energy levels were non-existent because of the ordeal she had been through. We all gathered around her to make things as easy and comfortable as we could. I got involved with household chores that I had never really done until then: cooking, hoovering and washing the floors - all the things Sally had done down the years as part of her normal day. I remember being in Sally's ward as the cleaners came in every day to wash and polish floors and thinking to myself, *I must take heed of what they are doing so that I will be able to do this, among other things, for Sally when she eventually comes home.*

I remember asking one lady how she washed the floors without leaving them soaking wet. She showed me how to wring out the mop so that it would be damp enough to clean the floors but also dry very quickly so that no one would slip on it. *Oh, how the mighty have fallen,* I thought to myself, but needs must, as they say, and necessity is the mother of invention, after all.

Another thing I caught onto was that, if I was doing chores that involved moving about the house, it was important to notice things along the way which needed my attention and do them as I passed them rather than having to retrace my steps later. 'Economy of movement' was what I referred to this exercise as. Sally said I was good craic; I didn't think it funny at all, but I certainly was happy to do whatever I could (and still am) to help make things easier for her.

On March 10th, 2000, a few days after Sally came home, the first of three eagerly-awaited grandchildren due to be born that year made an appearance; a beautiful girl. Stephen and Noreen named her Aoibheann. She was the first of what were to be three granddaughters who would each wind their way into our hearts, in their own special way. Catherine and Pat's daughter, Kate, was born in late March and Edward and Clare's daughter, Sarah, came in early May. After such a trying time for the McCallion household over that four-month period, this certainly was a time for celebrating and thanksgiving for the gift of new life and beginnings.

During the time of Sally's illness and recovery, Mammy had to go into one of the care homes for the elderly. She didn't like being there and neither did we. But we had no choice, as no one else could look after her. Sally made sure that I went to visit Mammy every day to make sure she had everything she needed to keep her comfortable. She couldn't go to see Mammy, she said, because she wouldn't be able to leave her there when visiting time was over, but she knew she wasn't fit to have Mammy at home with us just then. That's Sally for you. I asked her one day why she felt this way and her answer surprised even me:

'Johnny, I promised your Mammy that I would never put her into one of those homes, and I won't; as soon as I am on my feet, we will bring her home again.'

This Is Our Time

When Sally had the second crisis and lost her spleen, it was an awakening call for both of us: we realised how close she had come to death. Sally said the pain that morning was so bad she was convinced she wasn't going to make it, but that she was prepared to go, knowing in her heart that I would somehow manage. Now it was my turn to say to her, 'you're great craic, Sally', and she said again that she knew I would have been OK.

It was in those early days of Sally's recovery that I also remember her saying to me, 'Johnny, this is our time'. And so we made sure that it was. St Patrick's Day fell not long after she'd come home, so I decided I would take her to Letterkenny to see the parades. But the closest we could get to the town was about a mile away - there was no way she could have walked it. Rather than disappoint her, I suggested that we should go further beyond Letterkenny, so we set off in the Ramelton direction. To this day, I couldn't tell you where we ended up in Donegal, but we stopped at a pub in the middle of nowhere to get something to eat. When we went in we found that it was mostly local people who were there and they were having a great bit of fun, singing and playing traditional Irish music, which both of us love. Sally ordered a pot of tea and a round of sandwiches and I had a pint of beer and a round of sandwiches as well. I ate most of them (her appetite hadn't fully returned by then), but just being there together meant so much to us.

The lady behind the bar served Sally's sandwiches on a silver tray and provided a china cup and saucer for her to drink her tea from. We certainly couldn't complain about the welcome and service that we received from all in the pub that St Patrick's day, among the Hills of Donegal. It was done with song, music, lots of craic and a welcoming smile. What more could we have asked for? After a while, I could see that Sally was tiring, so I said it was time to go and asked the lady for our bill. She said we owed her three euro; I said she must be mistaken as we'd each had drinks and sandwiches so it must be more than that, but she said, 'I told you it was three euro, so it is three euro'. If only I could remember where that pub was. Ah well, it was a great day.

Another time, around the end of May or start of June, I said to Sally, 'would you like to go out for your tea tonight?' and, of course, her answer was, 'yes, why not?'

She was starting to recover her strength by then, so around six o'clock I said to her, 'let's go', and I put the dog's lead on him. She said, 'you can't take Deefer in to eat anywhere - they won't let you', and I said, 'they will where we are going'.

So off we went, and when I walked on by our car, which was parked in our driveway, that brought another question, 'where are we going?' and I said, 'just you wait and see'.

We meandered on our way at a pace that was comfortable for Sally until we came to a fish and chip van with a low wall around the front of it. I asked her what she would like to eat and she said, 'you have to be joking'; of course, I wasn't! It was as if we were teenagers again, without a care in the world, enjoying the simple things of life as we sat on that wall with Deefer between us, making sure he got his fair share from both of us - especially my battered sausages. That meal cost £5.50 and it is still one of the best meals I have ever had (and certainly better than the one we had in a local hotel some days later that cost us nearer £40).

Memories are made of times like these if we only take time to cherish them. This was followed by our first holiday since Sally took ill... well, our second attempt at having a break away from it all. We had booked a holiday to Lanzarote, at the end of May, but a few days before we were due to fly out there Sally was once again admitted into hospital. Her gallbladder had been causing her a great deal of pain, and, because of her history, the doctor decided not to take any chances, so in she went. She was released from hospital on the very day - and at the very time - that we should have been flying out from Belfast.

The following morning, I headed into town only to discover that most of the travel agencies were closed for the Whitsun holidays, but I only needed one to be open to solve our dilemma and I found one, luckily enough. While I was speaking to the young man in the travel agent's he told me that a cancellation had just come in but that we would need to be able to travel that Wednesday. It was for a two-week, all-inclusive break in Cyprus and it was nearly half of the original price. Of course, I booked it and off we set. It turned out to be everything we needed. We could stay by the poolside every day or dander at our leisure to two local beaches, or we could take a taxi into the nearest town and spend an afternoon at their beach. It was one of the best holidays we have ever had and it really was our time, with space for ourselves. I don't mean that to sound selfish, but it was just what we needed.

A year or so later, I was watching a TV programme called *Holidays from Hell* and couldn't believe my ears or eyes when the presenter named and shamed the very same hotel where we had spent our holiday in Cyprus as the focus of their ongoing investigations. It gave a totally damming report on every aspect of it, from the food to the type of clientele frequenting it. This proved to me that the circumstances and frame of mind that we have when we take a holiday can blind us to the reality of what is going on around us; I hope that makes sense to everyone reading this.

Ongoing Healing

One area of my life that I haven't yet mentioned in relation to this time of crisis with Sally's health is how my faith in God fared throughout it all. And believe me when I say; that is a whole different story. It would be fair to say that I wasn't on the best of terms with God during those six months from January until June. Looking back, I believe I went through the five stages of grief (just as people do when they suffer the loss of a beloved member of their family or close friend) because I did.

When I could, I would normally go to daily morning Mass; that is, under normal circumstances, but these were anything but. There was one morning, in particular, before Sally went into hospital for her operation that I was up earlier than usual. I couldn't sleep because of all the possible scenarios that were racing through my mind as to what may be the eventual outcome of this situation for us all. I was moving around our bedroom when Sally said, 'are you going to Mass, Johnny?'

My reply was, 'I don't even know if I am speaking to God at this moment, or even if I want to speak to Him, after all He has done to you'.

'Well,' said Sally, 'if you can't go for yourself, please go for me'.

So I went. I got into the chapel and knelt down, but I couldn't bring myself to say a prayer. Not a word; not even for Sally. There was a man in the row in front of me who I normally would have shied away from, as he had a habit of praying out loud. I always found this to be quite annoying as I liked to pray in a meditative way; silently within myself. Anyway, pray out loud he did. But this particular morning, something happened. I realised, whether he knew it or not, he was doing my praying for me as he meandered through his list of prayers for those who couldn't pray for themselves. I met a friend on my way out of Mass who asked about Sally. I related the above episode to her and said I knew that Sally would be OK again.

Obviously, prayer was very much to the fore since the day Sally was told she had cancer. While she was in theatre having her operation I was in an oratory praying in the presence of the Blessed Sacrament that all would go well for her. Because, since I was the innocent child in the womb of my birth mother, I have experienced how God had guided my every footstep and protected me from all that was not of Him, I have always felt a special connection with Him.

Why then, you may well ask, had I any problem praying for Sally? I have often thought of that question myself, and while it seems, at that time, I had lost any faith in Him, I have come to the conclusion that it was more about His faith in me than my faith in Him. After all, I am only human and He is divine. This is why I believe that the Jesus who I have come to love and believe in cannot be confined by the boundaries of our human thinking. I also believe that we limit the power of God by the limitations of our expectations of His power.

In September of that year, our world was to take another bad turn when I was made redundant. I would have seen it as a total disaster if it had happened before Sally took ill, but our priorities had changed dramatically over the last few months and we knew, without doubt, that good health was more important than any wealth or possession.

Around that time, a notice appeared in all parish bulletins asking people who would be interested in being trained as diocesan catechists to put their names forward for consideration. This I did, and I was successful. The training was to be carried out by a form of distance learning and would involve a lot of home study followed by essays on topics set by the Maryvale Institute in Birmingham. All of this was alien to me; I had left the college when I was fourteen to work in a local engineering factory because Mammy had been promised that I would get an apprenticeship after a few months. This never happened. The factory closed down a few years later and I had to make a career detour into sales, where I spent the rest of my working life, progressing from menswear to household furnishings and, finally, into the oil industry as a company representative.

It was a two-year course, and during the time I was studying, I was approached by my good friend, Sister Anna, who asked me if I would like to train as a spiritual director in Thornhill Convent. Manessa House in Dublin, where the training usually took place, was being closed for major renovations that year and she had been asked if she could organise it from here. It would last for seven or eight months and it would involve some reading as well as monthly residential workshops (from Friday to Sunday), with some written work thrown in as well. I laughed and said: 'You must be joking, Sister; I have enough studying and writing to do at present to last me a lifetime without taking on any more.' 'Johnny,' she replied, 'it will be no bother to you as there won't be that much work involved - you will do most of it during the residential weekends.' So I agreed to let my name go forward as a possible candidate for the course. At my interview I was asked would I be disappointed if I was not selected by the panel and I answered: 'Life has taught me that, if I want something and God doesn't want me to have it, then I won't get it, but it has also taught me that, if I don't want something and God does want me to have it, then have it I will. So I will leave it up to God to decide, and I will accept that.'

I certainly got the bug for learning more about my faith; after completing both of these courses, I decided to continue with some more distance learning. This time, a group of us focused on studying the catechism and we met once a week in the Thornhill Centre; I now have the complete course set by the Maryvale Institute. I remember Petroc Willey, one of the lecturers, saying, before we undertook to do the course, we would find the catechism to be one of the greatest love stories ever written. Well, I am sure you can guess what I thought of that statement, but he was proven to be right, as by the time we started the second unit it became obvious that there is a lot more to the catechism than the basic tenets we had drummed into us as children.

To me, it was as if we had been trying to bake a cake that never came out of the oven right... until someone pointed out that one of the main ingredients was missing. And so it was with the catechism that we had been taught. I often asked myself what was missing. Well, for me, I eventually identified the missing component as 'love'. What we had been taught had come from the head and for the head: by that, I mean that someone (or some group of people) decided to condense the original catechism into what it became after they had worked at it; and they had, of course, removed the heart. Life has taught me that the hardest journey we will ever make may also be the shortest: the one from the head to the heart. Another thing that struck me is that, in my younger days, the Church used to be referred to as 'Mother Church', and this is such a fitting phrase because, for me, it is in the softness of the mother's bosom where we will always find the heart.

As if all of this wasn't enough, I then ventured into scripture study with the Dominicans in Tallagh, Dublin; again, via the distance learning mode. I found that I did a lot of my reading, and indeed writing, in the early morning while others at home were still asleep. This, in turn, made it possible for me to play my part in the care for Mammy, which I hope was a help to Sally.

By this time, we had the support of three teams of carers coming in to help with Mammy's care. As far as we are concerned, they were a Godsend. They dealt with things in such a gentle and caring way and never once did they take away Mammy's dignity. In many ways, they helped not just Mammy, but also us, as they had a great way of making light of any situation.

Life moved along for all of us, especially Sally, who had had such a torrid start to the new millennium. She started to find her feet again (literally) but she was never the same as she was before her crisis, it is fair to say. Her confidence, dare I say it, was shook to her very foundations - even more so than her health.

In July of that year, Mary graduated from university, and by September she had started teaching in Gaelscoil Éadain Mhóir, a recently-established Irish medium school based in the Gasyard area of the Lecky Road - the street that had been so central to my younger days. Today, she is the principal of that school and I doubt you would find any prouder parents than us in the whole of Derry.

We had been blessed with the arrival of more grandchildren during those years. Stephen and Noreen had another daughter, Róisín, in 2001 and Edward and Clare had another son, Liam, in 2002. In 2004, Catherine and Pat had a son, Finn Brady, and Emmet and Michelle was blessed with a daughter Teagan, who arrived in 2005. Like all of our grandchildren, they have, simply by bringing their own colours, added to our picture of love.

Director Of All Directors

I said earlier that if I wanted something and God didn't want me to have it, then I wouldn't, but also that if God wanted me to have something that I didn't want, then I would have it. It was time to pray again as to where God wanted me to use these gifts He had bestowed on me and it was also time to let Him make it clear where He wanted me to do that.

The first thing that happened was that I heard of a man in our parish, Charlie Gallagher, who, like myself, was wanting to give back some of what he had received. He was a retired religious studies teacher and this seemed like a good fit. We met and discussed what our aims and objectives were and found that we had similar ideas. We decided to set up an adult faith support group in the Holy Family Church and got the use of the upper room for Wednesday evenings, from 8pm until 10pm. We also discussed the boundaries that must be in place so that each of us knew where we stood. First and foremost was that the whole area of confidentiality would be paramount to the foundation of the group. Secondly, we should only have one leader: Jesus Christ.

There would be no titles, as everyone who came to the group would be equal in all things and at all times. Thirdly, while we may not always agree with what another was saying, we would always respect them as a person.

Since our first meeting, we have always had the word of God on our prayer altar, accompanied by a picture of the Holy Trinity, a copy of the catechism and a lit candle to remind us of the presence of Jesus. The aim, or mission, of the group was to bring people to a point in their lives where they would be better informed about questions and answers relating to their faith. The objective was to bring them to a point where they could make informed decisions about their faith journey (rather than have a knee-jerk reaction) to any crises in their lives that may knock them off course.

In 2005, a good friend of mine, Martin Mc Laughlin, came under a lot of flak because he spoke out publicly on behalf of a young man who had been abused by a priest in the Derry Diocese after the BBC aired a programme in which they carried an interview with the then Bishop of Derry, Séamus Hegarty. Martin is the heart and soul of a youth group called Derry Search that was set up in Creggan during the '70s under the name 'Our Lady of Knock Youth Group'. The main aim of the leaders back then was to give the young people of the area something other than the ongoing Troubles to focus their energies on, while at the same time building up their self-esteem and confidence - which had been at rock bottom as a result of the lack of opportunities for work or for any kind of social advancement - as well as deepening their faith in God. As the name indicates, it is very much a faith-based group; both the adults and the young people are all searching for what is important to them as they travel along life's highway.

I had been attending a weekend seminar in Athlone Town (for those involved in the evangelisation mission of handing on the faith within parishes throughout Ireland) around the time the situation with Martin became public knowledge. A nun approached me while we were on a break and said that the situation in Derry was awful and that she wished Martin had come to her before he spoke out as she would have kept him right regarding how he should have handled the situation.

I asked her what her advice would have been and she said that he should have gone to the Bishop and discussed it with him rather than go public. She went on to tell me that there was a lot of wrong information being put out by people with their own agendas. There was no way, she said, that the Church had paid out the settlement agreed between the priest and his accuser, which was the story doing the rounds in Derry at the time. She knew for a fact, she said, that it was the priest's family who had given him said money, as they owned a shirt factory in Strabane. I told her I didn't know who had told her that, but that it wasn't true: the priest concerned came from a working-class background and his family didn't own any shirt factory in Strabane.

'So, Sister,' I said, 'someone else gave you wrong information to suit their agenda... of covering up the truth.'

I had left Search back in '96 and, as I mentioned earlier, it was a painful decision for me to make at the time. But I felt now was the time for me to return as I was the first layperson to be made aware of this abuse; Martin was the second. During a Search weekend we had been given a message, from a priest of the diocese that if we revealed any of what we knew, we would be committing the sins of calumny and detraction - which is punishable by excommunication. So I was the one person who could say, without a doubt, that what Martin was saying was the way it happened. I knew, once again, that God was showing me where He wanted me to be and (for now) with whom He wanted me to share the many gifts and blessings that He had bestowed upon me over the past nine years. That was the defining moment for me; I knew then and there (and without question) that I had to speak out and show my total support for Martin and the young man (referred to as 'Peter' in the press). And the best way to do that was to return to Search.

Let there be no doubt: my faith is only as strong as it is today because it is in God and God alone that I believe and trust. Because, if I was to let my thinking be influenced by what others have done to me and said about me personally since then, in the supposed name of God, then my faith would be totally non-existent. So, back I went and got totally involved in the Search group again. I didn't join the Search leadership committee, though, as I felt this was not the road God had chosen for me to journey.

On one occasion, when I was reflecting on my journey over the nine years I had been away from Search, I remembered something that had happened to me during a Search weekend the year before I'd left. I was standing at the back of the oratory during prayer time. The Blessed Sacrament was exposed, and silently, as I looked around at the young people, I was praying, *please Lord, don't ever let me lead one of these young people astray with wrong teaching,* because I had been overcome by the awesomeness of the responsibilities attached to my calling into the whole area of youth ministry. Immediately, in the silence of my being, a voice spoke and said, *I will feed you, as I need to use you in My name.* A peace that I knew could only have come from God came over me in that moment. I knew, there and then, that all would be well with me and God.

Then it hit me like a sledgehammer: this was why He had taken me away from Search in '96 - so that He could feed me. All of the courses that I thought I had taken by my own hand had all along been planned for me by my God, so that He could use me in His name. Once again, I had caused myself so much pain by trying to resist His call, and, once again, I had discovered (with the gift of hindsight after the event) that it was God who was doing the calling. At times, I have to remind myself that I wasn't the first this has happened to since the beginning of creation - and neither will I be the last. As I said, it isn't so much about my faith in God, but rather, it is all about His faith in me.

Moving On And Letting Go

The scriptural studies continued and I was very content with life at that time. Sally and I had settled into a routine, with Mammy's needs very central to every decision we made. If we wanted to go on holiday and nobody else was available to care for her, we had to make arrangements for her to go into a care home for whatever length of time we would be away; she didn't like that. Actually, that is a bit of an understatement - she hated it. It always took me a few days before I could start to enjoy the break without feeling guilty. It was only when we realised that the respite care wasn't just for Mammy, but also for us, that we got the full benefit of our free time. As we saw it, it was also beneficial for Mammy because we came back with our batteries fully charged.

Late on in the summer of 2006, just after we had come back from one such holiday, my brother Kevin rang me to tell me that, while we had been away, he had been diagnosed with bowel cancer. He would need an operation to have the growth removed, then a course of chemo. I had a friend who'd had bowel cancer himself several years before that. He had heard about Kevin's diagnosis and rang me, telling me Kevin should make sure that the bowel should be left exposed for at least a week after the operation. There was a danger, he said, that it could perforate. If that were to happen and the bowel wasn't exposed, there could be serious consequences. But Kevin said his consultant had told him he couldn't do this as he needed to get him stitched up and the wound healed as fast as possible so that they could get the chemo started; the tests had shown that the cancer had spread to his lung.

Kevin also said he didn't want Mammy to know there was anything wrong with him, so we would have to make up a story that would cover the real reason he wasn't calling in to see her over those next six weeks. He told me not to be coming to the hospital as we had enough to do caring for Mammy and that he would keep me up to date with all that was going on, one way or another.

He had his operation. During that first week, while he was still in the intensive care unit, there was a crisis. Kevin's consultant wasn't there that day and had left his houseman in charge. A nurse expressed concern about Kevin's condition but the doctors maintained they were in control of what was happening with him. But the intensive care nurse disagreed and she called in Mr Bateson, the general consultant, who diplomatically got them to review his symptoms again. This time, they realised what was happening and Mr Bateson then had to perform an emergency operation to rectify the situation as well as he could. Needless to say, Kevin's bowel had perforated. His insides had been poisoned, leading to the very serious consequences for him that my friend had warned us about. Kevin was left with permanent damage that meant a change of lifestyle that he certainly would not have chosen for himself. To add insult to injury, the cancer that Kevin was told was definitely in his lung turned out to be nothing more than scarring from an old childhood illness.

Around 2004, one of my best friends, Johnnie White, was diagnosed with lung cancer. I had gone with him to the hospital on the morning he'd had his x-rays done, and on the way out he said to me that something must be wrong because the radiologist asked if he had an appointment to see his doctor soon; when he said that he hadn't, she said maybe he should make one to get the results. He didn't even have to make that appointment; his doctor called down that evening to his home to confirm the news that he had been dreading: he had lung cancer. The doctor said they would give him a course of chemo to help reduce the tumour before (depending on the test results after chemo) removing part (or all) of his lung.

Johnnie's faith was truly inspirational throughout it all; never once did I hear him say that God had deserted him in his time of need. Just as I noticed with others who found themselves in similar situations to his, Johnnie, rather than lean on those around him, became the one to do the carrying as he reassured Doreen and their children that he would be OK. And, sure enough, he went from strength to strength. I know he amazed even his consultant, Rose Sharkey, because he told me that she commented on how strong his faith was during his ordeal. Five years after he was first diagnosed, Dr Sharkey told him she was delighted to be giving him the all-clear... only then revealing that his prognosis at the outset had been nine months.

Everyone was delighted, to say the least. But then, on September 25th, 2008, life took a cruel twist for the White family. Doreen and Johnnie had gone to the Northside shopping centre, in Shantallow, and had met Doreen's brother, Georgie. They went into the café there for a bite to eat before heading home to the bungalow they had bought just a few years before. The bungalow had been their life's goal and was a fresh challenge for Johnnie to renovate it into the home they both wanted at that time of their lives. Johnnie was amazing with his hands: unlike yours truly, he could undertake any type of work around the house and when he had finished the task at hand it would have been difficult to find any tradesman who could have done it better. That was the Johnnie I knew: a man of God, but always a man of the people, with his feet firmly on the ground and without airs or graces.

They got back home around midday and he told Doreen he was going to lie down for a while as he wasn't just feeling the best. Doreen went round to the local playschool to collect one of their grandchildren, who had just started and was only in for half a day. While she was gone,

Doreen's sister Bridie called to the house, where she found Johnnie in the bathroom being sick. When Doreen returned a few minutes later, Bridie met her at the door and told her about Johnnie. At this, Doreen insisted she would phone Johnnie's doctor. The doctor asked to speak to Johnnie, and when Johnnie came off the phone he announced that the doctor was sending an ambulance to take him straight to the hospital. He walked into the ambulance when it arrived, and as she had no one to watch the child (her sister had gone by this time) he told her not to worry; he would be back in an hour. Doreen then phoned one of their sons, Conal, and he went and met the ambulance at the hospital along with his wife Angela. After Johnnie was admitted, he told Conal to phone Doreen and tell her he was OK.

Conal had just gone outside to call her when Johnnie asked Angela to get him quickly; he wasn't feeling well. Johnnie died before Doreen had a chance to get over to him. It was a heart attack. He certainly was coming home an hour later, but not, I am sure, in the way that he meant when he uttered those prophetic words on his way out of their home just a short time before.

Not All Doom And Gloom

It may have seemed all doom and gloom for us at that time, and, in certain ways, it was, but life was ongoing in the background, producing its usual twists and turns. The grandchildren were all progressing at their own pace, each adding his or her own unique colour to our lives as they vied with each other for our love and attention.

I would always tell them (jokingly, of course) that I never made a difference between any of them; that I hated them all the same, none of them any more or less than the other. They are great young people, forging their way into the world, and Sally and I are glad we can say they are our grandchildren.

Life at this time certainly contained a lot of letting go, but there was also the gift of new life to help make up for the loss of those we loved. Between 2000 and 2005, we witnessed the births of seven grandchildren; such is the natural progression of life. Our own lives had certainly changed during this time. On August 30th, 2005, Sally and I celebrated our 40th wedding anniversary - a milestone that, at one time, we thought we wouldn't have. It was a time of great celebration and hope.

It was also a time of thanksgiving for the many blessings God had bestowed upon us - even for the ones we didn't see as blessings at the time. Once more, life took on a drive of its own and we just went with the flow, trusting that everyone would be OK. As I said earlier, the safety and welfare of our family is the most important goal in our lives and that is how it will be until the day God calls us home and beyond.

When I take time to reflect on the differences between our roles as parents and grandparents, it saddens me to think that, because of the everyday pressures we allowed society to put upon us as parents, our children may have missed out on the most important aspect of our mission, which (I now believe) was to give them our undivided attention.

For isn't that just another definition of the word 'love'? By that, I mean they should never have had any doubt that they (and they alone) were the centre of our world. They should never have had any fear or doubt of the depth of our love for them and they should always have known we would move heaven and earth to keep them safe from the ways of the outside world. Don't get me wrong; they were the centre of our universe. Everything we did, we did for them, because of our love for them. But now we had grandchildren, and without the pressures of having to provide for their daily needs, I could be much more relaxed with them.

We had so much more time to spend with them than we did with our own children in years gone by. The big difference was that we could fit into their day rather than them having to fit into ours; something our children had to do because of the need for us to go out and earn a living so that we could provide for their needs.

I loved nothing better than winding them up, and I suppose one of the biggest wind-ups I played on them was when I claimed I was the real Harry Potter and that the names of the main characters had been changed to protect their privacy because they were my grandchildren. When they were younger and they did not yet know my own story, I would tell them that, in time, all would be revealed. So on and on it went.

When it came to my 65th birthday I sent them each an invite and told them that, unless they had their invite with them, they would not be admitted into my party because I couldn't take the chance that some imposter would try to gatecrash it. The big day arrived, and as the party time approached, our daughter Catherine, who lives in Cork, came to me and said:

'You have really done it this time. Molly (Catherine and Pat's firstborn and our fifth grandchild, who was born on August 7, 1997) is in a panic as she has left her invite at home and now thinks she won't get into the party - you will have to print her out another one..'

Later at the party, my cake was brought in. It had my photo on it, which was taken when I was about 10 or 11 years old, and I was wearing those National Health-issue wire-framed glasses that everyone wore back then.

When our grandson Matthew saw the photo on the cake, he said, 'he really is Harry Potter!' I have many of these stories and great memories of my grandchildren, and they are all engraved on my heart. I just love the freedom of the relationship that I have with them all. Sally always says to me, 'will you stop teasing the wains; you are breaking their temper'.

To which I reply, 'well, they give as good as they get; what do you want me to do?'

Hopefully, their memories of us will be ones of laughter, great craic and lots of love.

All A Part Of Life

As we moved into 2008, little did I realise that Rose Kelly was once again about to intrude into my life; this time through a revelation from another branch of the Kelly clan hailing from Rose's native townland of Brackagh. A good friend of ours, Fr Peter Madden, who we first met in 1983 when he came to our parish in Derry as a newly-ordained priest, was celebrating his silver jubilee with a Mass of thanksgiving. We received an invite to join him in his new parish of Desertmartin, in the new church at the top of Iniscarn Road, and then afterwards in the local GAA hall for a bite to eat.

After the Mass, Sally and I went down to the adjoining graveyard to visit the graves. Two of Rose's sisters, Alice and Josie, and her brother Paddy were buried there. It is a small graveyard with several rows of family plots in it, and, while we were standing at Josie's grave, a lady came to Paddy's grave and Sally asked me if I knew who she was, to which I replied I didn't, but that I would soon find out. I wandered along the row, and when I reached Paddy's grave I asked her if she knew him. She told me that he was her father and asked why I was asking about him. Then I told her who I was and that I had found their graves twelve years ago when I was searching for Rose.

A man came along just then and she introduced him to me as her husband. Then another man passed by. As he did, they told him that I was Rose's son - a comment that he seemed to ignore, as he went on his way without speaking. This annoyed me a bit. *A bit?* It annoyed me a lot. Maybe, unbeknown to himself, he had hit a nerve with me; that of denial.

I decided if he was at the hall afterwards that I would approach him again and try to get to the bottom of the problem. When we reached the car park at the GAA hall and got out of our car, I saw the lady from earlier. She was talking to a group of people who were all looking in our direction. Obviously, she was filling them in on the events of our meeting. And it turned out that the woman she was talking to at the front of the group was her mother; Paddy's widow (who was another 'Rose Kelly', incidentally). This was to be the start of another chapter of my story. Arrogance and fear of the unknown are the things that come to mind when I try to recapture what my emotions were whenever I found myself in those types of situation. I needed to be strong and that is why I put on the mask of arrogance; it helped me hide the reality of the great fear of denial that lurked deep within my being.

Onwards I went to the hall and to my other mission, which was to get talking to the man who had passed me by while I was talking to Paddy's daughter Rosaline (that was her full name; another derivation of the 'Rose' name) at the grave. I knew he was one of the Moran family but I couldn't understand why he seemed to ignore me earlier. It was his mother, Tessie, who had welcomed me so warmly into the family clan some nine or ten years before. But it turned out he had a hearing problem, and was, in fact, quite open when I approached him. Turning to his wife, he made what was, for me, a revealing statement:

'Ann, this is Patsy's half-brother'.

Half-brother? My ears pricked up at that one. How much more was known about me that hasn't been told yet? That was the big question.

On a lighter note, I went as the designated driver to Fr Peter's celebration so that Sally and our friends, Eileen and Eamon Walker, would be free to have an alcoholic drink. But there was no drink at the hall. They decided to get one on the way back home, but that wasn't to be, either; the pubs along the way were already closed. The best-laid plans of mice and men will always go astray.

During Easter week of 2009, my brother Kevin came to me and said he had to go into hospital for further tests. He was having trouble with his throat and needed to have it checked out just in case the cancer had returned. Again, he told me he didn't want me to tell Mammy about it and I knew it must be something serious when he said that. Kevin went into hospital; the news wasn't good. I was to find this out when a friend of mine, who I met up with at our weekly parish meeting, said to me that she was very sorry to hear the bad news about Kevin.

'What bad news?' I asked her.

She nearly died as I again asked, 'what bad news?'

Then she told me she had been told his cancer had returned.

I couldn't get into the hospital to see Kevin that evening because visiting time had been and gone by the time I heard the news. It was a very long night. I was desperate to find out what was going on and, to top it all, we still couldn't tell Mammy what was happening.

She didn't even know that he was in hospital because that's the way Kevin wanted it to be. When I got in to see him the following morning, he told me the doctors needed to do more tests to help them discover what stage the cancer had reached (it was in his thyroid this time) but that this would take several days to sort out. I was in touch with him every day, keeping up to date with what was happening and hoping beyond hope that his cancer would be one of the types that could be managed or cured. Sadly, Kevin's cancer was the kind that the doctors couldn't do anything about other than keep it at bay for as long as they could. To add insult to injury, it wasn't secondary cancer from his bowel cancer but another one altogether. How unlucky can anyone be?

Now we had to tell Mammy. We had no choice; the wagons were gathering and we had sheltered her for as long as we could from all that he was going through (and, indeed, had gone through previously when he first took ill). She was devastated, to say the least. Words cannot describe the grief that hit her at that time. She kept saying, 'why him, why my Kevin, why not me?'

Sally and I had already booked to go to Poland for a few days in early May. Kevin warned me we were not to cancel the break as we needed it so we would be able to continue to look after Mammy.

Things progressed at an alarming rate over the next few weeks. He had great difficulty swallowing and speaking so he had to go to theatre to have a procedure done to relieve his discomfort. This resulted in him losing his voice, and if you knew Kevin, you would know that this was one of the worst things that could have happened to him.

He was such an outgoing character; so full of life and fun. He loved holding the floor when he was in company and loved being the centre of attention - and, by God, did he lap it all up.

During this time, I felt it was my privilege and honour to be Kevin's brother. This is something no one on earth can ever take from us. He was, and will always be, my 'wee' brother Kevin - all six foot three or four of him. He didn't want anyone to know that he was smoking and asked me if I would bring cigarettes over to him, so I did. He knew I was anti-smoking but I knew they couldn't do him any more harm, and, if anything, they probably made the whole situation a bit more bearable, if that was possible. I still have the last open packet of fags that he gave to me to keep for him, along with his lighter, when I picked him up from the hospital one Saturday morning to take him home for the weekend.

One morning (this was before he lost his voice) he asked if I could get him a priest so that he could make his peace with God. I didn't hesitate and when I brought them together I said, jokingly, 'I'll see the both of you in a couple of hours, boys'. It meant so much to me that Kevin would place his trust in me to do this for him at such a special time in his life.

Just before we went to Poland, Kevin was transferred to the City Hospital, in Belfast, for further treatment. On the last day of our holiday, I got a phone call from Mary telling me that Kevin wasn't doing so well.

It's lucky we were leaving the following morning because I just had to get home ASAP. We flew into Belfast and went straight to the hospital, worried as to how we would find him, but I should have known better: despite the seriousness of the situation, he was dealing with it in his usual manner - by making light of it.

There he was, lying in a bed that wasn't big enough for him (his feet were pushing over the end of it) and he looked up as Sally and I entered, lifted a pen and notepad and wrote something on it before handing it to me.

The note read, *You are a bit too early for the wake.* How could you answer that one, other than laugh? That's my wee brother: no one can ever take away memories like that from me; no one.

Finally, Kevin was transferred back to the Foyle Hospice in Derry as nothing more medically could be done for him. The people in the hospice were best equipped to care for him on his final earthly journey. We had to make special arrangements to bring Mammy down to see Kevin as we knew that he wasn't going to be with us for much longer. Much as we wanted to protect her, we also knew that she needed to see him. It turned out to be one of the most special memories that I have of our time together.

Bishop Daly, who himself was retired and had taken up a pastoral role in the hospice, had asked me to let him know when Mammy would be coming to see Kevin so that he could make sure he would be there to meet her. He just didn't meet her; he accompanied her on what I am sure was the most painful journey Mammy had ever undertaken in her life. When we brought Mammy to the hospice, Bishop Daly was waiting, as promised, to meet us. He led us all into Kevin's room and remained there with us. After a short prayer of thanksgiving was said, he suggested we should all leave Mammy alone with Kevin for a while. As we were walking out of the room I turned to Bishop Daly and asked him if he would stay in with them. He did.

It was only later, as I reflected on this, that I thought to myself that this was Kevin and Mammy's Calvary; Bishop Daly was their John. Not a word was spoken and the room was palpable with the love of the mother for the son and (need I say it) the love of the son for his mother. As I said, Bishop Daly didn't just meet Mammy that day: he accompanied her and Kevin on their journey to Calvary.

Kevin deteriorated rapidly after that. My final act was to ask him if I could say a decade of the Rosary with him and he asked me if he was dying. When I say asked me, I mean he lipped the words. As I spoke the words of the prayers, we held hands and looked at each other. When we finished, he mouthed the words, 'I love you, Johnny', and I said that I loved him. It was the last time I saw Kevin alive and I feel so privileged that we had that very special time together.

Kevin died on May 23rd, 2009; a date etched in my memory. My wee brother was gone, never to return.

What Next?

Mammy was never the same after Kevin died. I prayed that God would take her out of the situation (a situation that no parent should have to go through) though, of course, it wouldn't be in my time, but God's. Once again, because of our caring for Mammy, we didn't have any time to grieve the loss of Kevin; Sally and I just got on with it. I honestly don't know if I could have done it without her. She is certainly a Godsend and not just my wife. We were soon to realise that it wasn't without cost to our own health; within six months of Kevin's death I was diagnosed with COPD and, in October 2010, Sally was struck down with pneumonia.

While Sally was laid up, as they say in Derry, Mammy herself was taken ill and had to be admitted to hospital. On the day she went in I didn't get back home until after seven in the evening, and then got a call from my niece Ann, in Gulladuff, to tell me that her father, Patsy, was very ill and wasn't expected to make a recovery from this illness. Patsy died on October 29th, 2010, and it was while I was at his funeral mass that another bit of the jigsaw fell into place. As Fr Paddy Baker offered his and the parish's condolences to Patsy's family, he named us all individually, starting with his wife Philomena, then his children, and finally us; his brothers and sister. For the first time since I had started my search into my birth background, the penny dropped. *Because I acknowledge that I am part of this family,* I thought, *it doesn't mean I am betraying Mammy and Daddy or Nuala, Kevin and Marian.* It had only taken me fourteen years to get to this point in my journey.

The question now was, what more did I have to open myself up to? What more was locked away in a place known only to me? And what more had I to take out of the locker? *Only God knows the answer to those questions,* I thought, *and I am sure He will provide them when the time is right.* I didn't have too long to wait for the answer to that one, because Patsy had asked to be buried back at the old Keenaght graveyard with his grandparents, Francis and Rose Kelly. This was the Kelly grave I had found on that first day I went to the Draperstown/Desertmartin area, in search of my hidden past, way back in 1996. Jimmy and I had been asked to do the first lift of Patsy's coffin along with Patsy's son Damien and his grandson, Conor. What I hadn't realised was this meant we would be carrying Patsy into and out of the chapel and then to his final resting place. Later, as we stood over the open grave and peered into it as we lowered Patsy's remains down, the thought that struck me was, *all that is hidden in the dark has been revealed in the light.* It certainly was being revealed in the light, because here stood two of the family's biggest secrets (me and Jimmy) in full view of all who were gathered there. How our Rose must have rejoiced in that moment, her secrets no longer hidden.

Edward, Stephen and Emmet had gone with me that morning for Patsy's funeral and I was very proud to have them supporting me. Mary had gone down to Kerry earlier that weekend to the All-Ireland Fleadh and Catherine couldn't get up from Cork in time for the funeral. Afterwards, I had to head back to Derry as Mammy was still in hospital and Sally still recovering at home from the pneumonia. It was a very busy and stress-filled day, but, with God's help, we all got through it.

Mammy wasn't showing any great signs of improvement but the doctors said she wasn't in any immediate danger of dying. They said they would keep me informed if there was any change in her condition. Of course, I was keeping my sisters Nuala and Marian informed of the situation by the day. Sally was improving slowly but she was annoyed because she hadn't been able to go to the hospital to see how Mammy was doing for herself. The week seemed to drag on and on. Then, in the early hours of November 9th, the hospital nurse rang and said we should come over; there had been a change in Mammy's condition. Sally insisted she was coming with me. Even though I was worried about her I didn't put up any resistance - not that it would have mattered, because when Sally makes up her mind to do something, she will do it. It was a long night. Nurses and doctors were in and out of Mammy's room but nobody was really saying much. The main priority seemed to be to keep Mammy pain-free and comfortable. They told us the consultant had decided to send her for further tests and x-rays in the hope of finding out what was going on with her. They also said he would be in when he was on his rounds, after nine o'clock, to talk to us. Mary called to the hospital on her way to school as she sensed something was wrong.

At some point that morning I convinced Sally to go home for a rest. Shortly after she left, the house doctor came to see Mammy. I was sitting outside her ward when the lady doctor came out and straight to where I was sitting. She knelt down beside me and started to tell me that the consultant wouldn't be able to see us until after three that afternoon but that, in her opinion, it would be very unfair to put Mammy through any further tests. It was then that the panic set in; I asked her straight to tell me if Mammy was dying as I had two sisters in England who would need to be told straight away if that was the case. She told me she was, but that they would do everything possible to make sure she wouldn't suffer, saying again that the consultant would bring us up to date with the situation later in the afternoon. Sally returned shortly after (she wasn't able to sleep when she went home) and I told her what was happening; she asked me to go home for a few hours' rest. Conor, our grandson, had to come over for an appointment later and he would need me to bring him over, anyway.

I had just reached home when my mobile rang. It was Sally (déjà

222

vu; we have been here before) saying that I should return as there had been a further change in Mammy's condition. It was one of the longest journeys I have ever made, not because of traffic or any delays but simply because of the panic within me. Part of me felt that I would be too late - if I wasn't too late already.

I was. Mammy, as I suspected, had passed away with only Sally in the room with her.

Afterwards, Sally said she was sorry she had talked me into going home when she did. I remember saying to her: 'Sally, did it ever strike you that Mammy may have found it very difficult to let go if I had been there when she was dying? You did everything for Mammy in the later years of her life so why shouldn't you have been the one who accompanied her on her final journey back to Daddy?'

We took Mammy back to the family home in Inishowen Gardens where we had found a love beyond all understanding. It was what she would have wanted us to do. I spent the first night of the wake alone with Mammy, surrounded by memories of so many happy times growing up there and of the people who helped make me the person that I am today. The house echoed with the voices of those long gone: my Ma and Da, uncles Johnny and Alex, my aunts Kath and Rose and lastly - but certainly not least - my Daddy, my brother Kevin and, now, my Mammy. Nuala and Michael came from their home in Hampshire, as did Marian and her husband Michael and their boys from Cornwall. It couldn't have been an easy journey for any of them.

It is well documented in the earlier pages of this book just how much I loved Mammy and Daddy. My love for Mammy was still every bit as deep as it was back then, but at the time of her death I was filled with relief that she was finally free of her living hell. Once again, as I did when Daddy, Kevin and, indeed, Patsy died, I didn't take time to grieve her passing. It wasn't until the first anniversary of her death that the enormity of my loss finally hit; I was devastated.

Time Out

As well as dealing with the emotional impact of Mammy's death, there was also the little matter of sorting out her belongings and arranging the sale of the family home. All of this took almost a year and caused us a lot of anguish at times. It wasn't just a house that was being sold; it was our home. Mixed in with all this was my own personal journey and how I was dealing with the loss of Mammy. I found I had to keep focused on what was right for me, otherwise, I found myself wandering off course and losing direction, and, indeed, losing interest in the things and people that mattered to me.

During this time, another one of my birth brothers died: the other John. Ironically, he was much the same age as Kevin; another young man struck down by cancer in the prime of his life. I got word of John's death on the morning of Saturday, September 10th, 2010, just as my own boys and I were clearing the last remnants out of our family home in Creggan.

A month before he died, Jimmy and I had made the journey back to Filey to see John, as we (and he) knew he wouldn't be with us for much longer. It was my first time back there since 1996 and it was lovely to have the chance to spend time with him and Kath, but also very poignant. While Jimmy and I were visiting Rose and Ted's grave we had a strange experience: a white feather floated down from the sky and rested on the ground between us, on top of the grave. When both of us looked up to the clear blue sky, there wasn't a bird to be seen for miles. A sign from heaven? I would like to think so. Now we had to make the journey again to say our final farewells to John.

All these things were in the mix as I tried to come to terms, once again, with the hand of cards life had dealt me. The issue that most concerned me was the Search youth group. I found that, as I was drained physically, mentally and, indeed, spiritually, I couldn't fulfil my role with them as I should have been doing. I prayed for God to guide me and show me what to do. It was then I remembered something that had been said at a guidance course I had attended once: that we should always take time out after any great trauma in our lives - especially after the death of a loved one. This was to give us time and space to renew our energies and time to come to terms with one's own change of circumstances.

There is a lot of wisdom in that way of thinking, for this is what we must do in order to be fully focused on the needs of those people with whom we have been called to share a very sacred space, without any worldly distractions on our part. I came away from Search at that time because I knew, in my heart, I owed it to them to take this time out and recharge my batteries. It turned out I never went back; God had other plans for me.

God's Faith In Me

L ife has taken me down some roads that I would rather not have travelled, but when I look back on the twists and turns of it all I realise there has been a purpose to them all. So, the question is: *Who am I and why am I here?* Followed by, *am I going about this life in the right or wrong way?* And, finally, *how will God judge me?*

One of the things I have come to believe is that my faith journey isn't so much about my belief in God; it is all about His belief in me. I say this because, as I reflect on my life journey, I clearly see the times that I turned my back on Him (and they were many) but never has He turned his back on me. I have come to realise that my joy is His joy and my pain is His pain because He has clearly promised that He would be with me (and everyone else) always; even until the end of time. Therefore, when I do come face to face with Him, I hope our final meeting as I leave this earth will go something like this: 'Come home, true and faithful servant. Many a mistake you made along the way, but at least you tried your human best to do My will.'

At the end of May 2012, I went over to Brackagh for the annual blessing of the graves. In many ways, it was my annual pilgrimage to the grave I happened upon by chance in my search for answers to my many questions regarding my birth background. As usual, all the Kellys from Brackagh and Gulladuff were there. As we were leaving the graveside after the blessing had taken place, Patsy's son Damien said to me,

'Johnny, I would love to know more about the woman in the grave'.

He was, of course, referring to Rose's mother, who had died in 1927, just over eighty-five years before.

Without thinking, I shot back at him: 'Damien, be careful what you ask for because you might just get it'.

Prophetic words or what? I do not know, but by July of that year, things took an amazing turn regarding his statement. I was mucking about on the computer, typing in different Kelly names in the hope that I might uncover some unknown part of Rose's story.

I had just typed in *Alice Kelly, Draperstown,* when a posting appeared halfway down the Google page; it was from a man in Missouri. He went by the name of Dan McClernon and he was researching the birth family of his maternal grandmother, Agnes (née McGuckin). His information was very scant: she had a sister, Rose, who had married a Francis Kelly who had bought the family farm from her father, Joseph McGuckin. Other than that, he had no further details.

I checked my copy of the 1911 census that I had for the McGuckin family that Rose's mother came from and, lo and behold, Joseph, along with Rose's and Agnes', names appeared on it.

Agnes was the youngest of the children. I thought to myself, this couldn't be the same family, but decided to reply to him anyway. Sure, the devil hates a coward. Within a few hours, I got a reply from Dan, who said he was delighted to hear from me but he wasn't sure that it was the same family. But he would like to keep in touch if I didn't mind.

I filled Dan in with all I had discovered about the family and explained how I was connected to them through my birth mother, Rose. Within a few days, Dan sent me a copy of a photo that was among his grandmother's memorabilia. It was of a young girl; she had signed her name *Rose B Kelly.* He wasn't sure who she was, but my heart jumped a beat; I knew I had seen that signature before. It was on a document that Rose had signed when she gave Jimmy up to his family in Coleraine. I asked Sally if she thought it was the same signature and she had no doubt that it was. I let Dan know who the young woman was but he was still in doubt that I was talking about the family he was researching.

Then he sent another photo, which had been taken when his grandmother made her one and only visit back to Ireland in 1960. Again, I was taken aback, because when I looked at this photo, I knew that, once again, I had seen her before... in the only photo I had of Rose (until now).

It had been given to me by Rose's oldest sister, Tessie Moran, on the night I first met her. It was a family group: Tessie standing to one side of her mother, who had the twins sitting on her knees (Rose and her sister May).

To the other side was her brother John, then to the rear stood Francis Kelly, and to his left stood their two aunts; her mother's sisters. I didn't know their names but this small, old, battered and torn photo from the early 1920s was to prove the key that unlocked the mystery of Dan's maternal grandmother's family history.

I put the photo Dan had sent me beside the one Tessie had given me. Although there had been a gap of forty years or so between the two being taken, there was absolutely no doubt that one of the ladies in the back row was indeed Dan's grandmother, Agnes. I immediately sent Dan a copy of my photo, suggesting to him that this lady was indeed his grandmother.

Within one hour of me emailing it to him, Dan had sent me a perfect copy of my old battered and torn photo; the very same picture was among his grandmother's memorabilia. Coincidence or God-incidence?

You can make up your own mind on that one but I have no doubt as to what I believe. Dan's search for his maternal grandmother's relations had ended, and I am happy to say our friendship had begun.

I shared, in detail, the story of my search into my birth background by sending him copies of my diary entries over a space of time. In turn, Dan sent me copies of his grandmother's letters from Ireland to her then boyfriend Hugh McClernon after he had gone to America to work for his uncle in Missouri. Then he followed up by sharing her letters to him when she herself went to Philadelphia on January 15th, 1920.

I felt honoured to be privy to what, for me, was a very sacred story of two young people from times gone by. Her letters gave me an insight into people long gone; people who had lived through hard times but who'd had the courage and the determination to face up to the trials of the day and to overcome them, in a way that we wouldn't have if we had been alive back then.

We had built up such a good rapport, Dan and me, that we decided to join together to do any subsequent family research where our interests may coincide. This resulted in the discovery of a branch of our extended families; the Lyons of Philadelphia.

We uncovered the heart-rending story of Patrick and Mary (Mary's maiden name was McGuckin and she was a sister of Rose's mother) and the tragic losses they endured. Six of their young family died during the Spanish flu epidemic of 1918-20; two of them on the same day.

Ever since then, Dan and I have stayed in constant contact by email and keep one another up to date with the latest news from our respective sides of the Atlantic. I will be eternally grateful to him because of the wonderful gift he gave me by sending me that family photo.

Thanks to him, Rose touched into my life in a way that I never would have imagined: she revealed to me what she had looked like as a beautiful young woman.

A Time To Celebrate

I was fast approaching my 70th birthday, which was to fall on December 15th, 2012. In my heart, I knew that others would be deciding to mark it in some special way. Anyone who knows me also knows that I don't do birthdays with any great gusto or enthusiasm as it brings up painful memories from my past.

Sally and I were on holiday in early September, and as we were sunning ourselves at the beach I said: 'Sally, I know that you crowd will be making surprise plans for my 70th, but would you do me a favour and let me do the planning?'

To which she replied, 'what plans?' Cheeky so and so.

I laughed and went on to explain that I had been thinking about it for a while, and would really like to take Sr Bernadine up on her suggestion, from my journey in '96, when she said, 'Johnny, when you think the time is right to have a Mass said for Rose, feel free to come back to the Nazareth House to have it'.

The problem with that was that I could never have had a Mass for Rose without having included Mammy and Daddy, and they would not have felt comfortable attending such a Mass. I had never taken her up on that offer for that reason, but now, I felt, the time was right. It must be a Mass of Thanksgiving for the gifts all three of them were (and still remained) to me and mine. That was how I came to organise my own 70th.

It honestly turned out to be the best birthday I'd ever had; not because of the presents but because of the *presence*. And by that, I mean the people who came to the celebration and added to the occasion by their presence. Among them were my immediate family, obviously, our friends, old and new, and then my relations from 'across the mountain', as I liked to refer to them. I was able to publicly acknowledge the role Rose had fulfilled in my life. I was also able to speak of the sacrifices Mammy and Daddy had made as they showed, not only me, but Nuala, Kevin and Marian, what God's love was all about. They knit us into a family unit that no one (except ourselves) could break, and, hopefully, that would never happen. Central to the joy of the occasion was the fact that our children and grandchildren all took part in the beautiful thanksgiving Mass, with Sally doing a fantastic job, as only Sally can, of narrating the presentation of the offertory gifts. Patsy's son, Damien, did one of the readings and his youngest daughter, Geraldine, also read one of the bidding prayers (she told me to include that). So it was truly a family celebration, in every sense of the word.

Then we headed down to the Gasyard on the Lecky Road for a wee bite to eat. I was delighted we had been able to get this venue for my party as it is on the street where I spent many of my early years, when I first came to Mammy and Daddy, in the home of my maternal grandparents, Kitty and Eddie McCourt. It is also only a stone's throw from the home of my paternal grandparents, Johnny and Mary McCallion, up in Beechwood Street.

I don't think I stopped smiling all that day (to this day I smile any time I think about it) simply because I was among most of the people who had helped make me the person I am. I just hope they were pleased with how I turned out.

From there, it was onwards and upwards as the younger generation started to emerge from their childhood years and into their teenage years and beyond. Marie, our first-born grandchild, was by now twenty years old and studying at university for her degree. Caoimhe, Matthew and

Conor were all progressing through their respective grammar school years and the others were all in primary school. Our youngest daughter, Mary, who had graduated from university in 2003 and who had started teaching in an Irish medium school, had, over the years, risen through the ranks so quickly that she was one of the youngest principals in the north of Ireland at the time of her appointment. So, who are the proud parents and grandparents, then?

Life had settled down to a gentle pace for Sally and me; after the loss and turmoil of the early years of the 21st century, we were very happy to enjoy this time and all it promised.

Another Milestone In Life's Journey

S ally isn't big into birthday parties, so when she reached her seventieth we had great difficulty in getting her to have a party at all. Not for her are surprise parties; I knew not to even go there as it would have caused her far too much stress and that would have ruined her special day. She agreed to have a gathering of those closest to her in our own home, so that is what she had. It ended up with Sally entertaining the younger ones, playing one game after another with them.

I knew that a bigger problem lay ahead: we were fast approaching our 50th wedding anniversary, which was to fall on August 30th, 2015, and Sally wouldn't want to be centre stage of the festivities for that, either. But I also knew we couldn't not celebrate such a special occasion; especially as, at one time, it looked like we wouldn't even be celebrating our 40th.

With the help of our own wains (four of them approaching their fifties themselves), we put the plans in place and kept Sally informed of everything so that she wouldn't be too stressed out about it all. We had our 50th thanksgiving Mass in St Mary's Church in Creggan (the church we were married in, by the late Fr Denis Mc Connellogue) and two very good friends of ours, Fr Joe Gormley and Fr Peter Madden, concelebrated the Eucharist for us on this extraordinary occasion.

Earlier in the year, I had come across a posting from the Chicago diocese in America, from the Archbishop himself, in which he invited all couples in the diocese who were celebrating their 50th wedding anniversary that year to a special diocesan celebration of married life; they just had to fill out the attached form. As I had been in Chicago in 1965 (albeit for just a few days) I decided to fill it in and ask them to remember us at their celebration, simply because they had set Sunday, August 30th for the occasion.

Little did I think that they would react to my email in the way they did. On the form, they had asked the participants to include two pictures of themselves - one from the time of their wedding, if they had one, and then one of them as they were now - as well as answer a few questions regarding what they thought had made their marriage special to them.

I did this, and not only did we get a reply from them thanking us for submitting the form, they also asked if they could include our details in the brochure.

Of course, we said we would be delighted if they did. Just before our anniversary, we received - much to our surprise - a box in the post with a Chicago postmark. It contained the brochure, which featured our photos and the statement we had included with the application.

There was also a scroll of the Archbishop's special blessing, with our names on it, which was being given to all of those taking part in Chicago. Later, we received a report of the goings on at the event and we discovered that they had prayed for us at their Mass, just as we had prayed for them at ours.

Sally and I did the readings at our Mass, our children did the bidding prayers and our grandchildren formed the choir. Catherine was the narrator for the offertory procession. We renewed our marriage vows surrounded by our children and my sisters, Nuala and Marian, who were the only two of our original wedding party still living, as Sally's brother Stephen and her cousin Celine had both passed away by then. I know she would have felt their absence deeply, as well as that of her brother

Michael, who sadly passed away on July 21st, 2013.

The ceremony to renew our vows was the most important part of the celebration for me, as we were surrounded by those who meant so much to us but also by those who had gathered with us in St Mary's, all of them there to be our witnesses.

Afterwards, we retired to a local hotel for a celebratory meal and an evening of song and dance. The young (and not-so-young) took part in the entertainment, with a few of the younger generation showing off their God-given talents, regaling us with their amazing singing.

I remember thinking, at the time, that the Derry diocese should take a leaf out of Chicago's book and celebrate the importance of lasting marriages by inviting couples like us, who are celebrating their 50th wedding anniversary, to come together, in these times of disposable partnerships, to promote the sacredness of marriage.

The Gift That Never Stops Giving

Dan McClernon (the grandson of Rose's aunt, Agnes) and I had kept up our contact on a regular basis, discussing all sorts of things, such as the weather on both sides of the Atlantic, the ongoing world situation and how our family members were all doing.

Just when I thought I had gotten everything relating to Rose that I could from Dan, another posting arrived from him, in late 2015 or early 2016, which included some more photos from Agnes' collection.

Among them was a photo of a lady with young two girls by her side. The girls were obviously twins. When I contacted Dan, I asked if he knew who they were, saying I hadn't realised they, too, had twins in their family.

Dan's reply dumbfounded me: he told me they'd never had twins in his family and explained that the lady in the photo was Rose McGuckin/ Kelly and that the girls at her side were her twin daughters, Rose and May. I was speechless. It was when I looked closer at the photo that the penny dropped: this may well have been the last photo they had taken together before Rose's mother died. I say this because, to look at her, the woman in the photo was obviously not keeping well, and also because the girls in the photo just reached up to her shoulder; they were just coming up to their eighth birthdays when she died in May of 1927.

My conversation with Patsy's son Damien, as we came away from Brackagh on that May evening the year before, came back to me then:

'Johnny, I would love to know more about the woman in the grave.'

'Damien, be careful what you ask for because you just might get it.'

By God, did he get it. And I have no doubt: it was by God's intervention that we got to know more about the woman that lay in the grave in the old Keenaght cemetery.

A New Journey Begins

In early 2016, our Mary made a life-changing announcement; not just for her, but for our whole family. It would lead to a lot of soul-searching for Sally and me as her parents. She told us that, following a public appeal from the local childcare agency, she had decided to express an interest in being an adoptive parent. She wanted to know what we felt about it all.

The process would involve her going through a very thorough interview process followed by an intense training course organised by the board. Then she would have to face a final interview with the adoption panel. Even after all this, they could make the decision that she wasn't suitable to be an adoptive parent.

There were several points that concerned us - not least was the possibility of the utter devastation that Mary would have to face if she wasn't approved by the board. What would that do to our beautiful, caring daughter? How would she be able to accept the rejection and how would she be able to pick up the pieces of her life afterwards? These were the minus points in the process and we had to balance them against the plus points, the strongest of those being her totally unselfish decision to venture down this path at that stage of her life.

This hesitation (especially on my part, of all people) may sound strange to anyone who is aware of my own story, but the difference this time was that I was watching my child make a major decision that would change her life forever.

We each had Mary on one hand and the unknown child on the other, and when we weighed up the situation regarding both, the scales were evenly matched.

Mary was a young woman who had always been very focused on what direction her life should take. Whatever important goals she set her mind on, she had mostly been successful in her pursuit of them. I am sure that, at times, she has, like the rest of us, suffered her disappointments, but she has dealt with them and got on in life. As a young woman approaching any major crossroads in her life, she has always been very focused (and indeed, driven) on what road she has wanted to follow.

The first time I really became aware of this trait in Mary was when she was making the first big decision regarding the career she wanted to go into. Teaching was her decision, but not just any teaching: she wanted to be a teacher in an Irish medium school. These schools really were in their infancy at that time, but despite her mother's protestations and my own hesitancy that there wouldn't be many jobs going when she graduated, Mary persisted, and train for this she did.

When she graduated, I left her down to a wee school in the Gasyard, here in Derry, for her interview. As I waited for her to return I looked around the site.

The school was a cluster of huts and there didn't seem to be any great atmosphere about the place. I thought to myself, *oh my God, what is she doing?* She returned some time later, interview over, and said to me, 'that's where I want to teach'. She got the job in the school and has since risen to be principal there. I must say, as parents, we are very proud of her and all that she has achieved in life. We are particularly proud of all the good she has done for the children, who have been blessed to have her as an aunt, a teacher and a principal, but, most of all, as a friend and mentor in their young lives.

That was on the one hand. On the other hand, we had a child who we knew absolutely nothing about. What we did know is that any child within the system wasn't there because of anything that they had done; they were there because of circumstances beyond their control.

They may have come from a broken home, a broken relationship or because their parent (or parents) found themselves unable to cope with the baby. Then again, they may have been in the system because the social workers had recommended they be taken from the parent(s) because of their unsuitability to care for a child. In all these situations, the child was blameless (and indeed, helpless) to do anything to help improve their home background. I only hope, as I relate the things that were going through my mind at this time, I haven't caused offence to anyone who is reading this.

I haven't touched on the biggest reason why I think the child should be given every consideration by the prospective adoptive parent, or parents, before they make their final decision on whether to adopt or foster a child or not. To put it simply, at one stage of my life, I was that child. I know how the decision made by Mammy and Daddy all those years ago to adopt, not just me, but my brother Kevin and sisters Nuala and Marian, had such a profound effect on each of us. We four came from different backgrounds and came along at different times, but we had all come with the same simple need: to have someone in our lives who could, and would, show us love beyond all understanding. Mammy and Daddy, in their unselfish act of bringing us together and then knitting us into a family, showed us that love; and, by God, it was a love beyond measure.

How could the unknown child not have the winning hand in this situation? And so, though we still had the concerns any loving parents would have for their child (because that is who Mary is: one of our five children, and she always will be), we gave her our every blessing and backing for the road she was about to go on. That backing came from everyone in our wider family as well.

The process seemed to go on and on. Even Sally and I had to be interviewed by her case worker and had to fill out a questionnaire about how we saw our role within the process. Just as our interview was coming to an end, the lady asked us if we were happy for Mary. Sally said that she was and, without thinking, I said I was happy for the baby because I knew the difference Mary's decision would make to her or him.

Then, in early November, Mary announced she had been given the date for her interview with the pre-adoption panel. She had told Sally the date before me, but, when she did tell me, I was stunned, to say the least. Being a leap year, there were 366 days in 2016. The panel had set her interview for December 15th at 12.45 pm. My birthday; an omen or what?

If I thought the announcement of the panel interview was nerve-wracking (albeit in a strange, nice way), it had nothing on the actual day itself. I had taken out a small piece of paper that I had been given when I was researching my own birth background. It had been photocopied from a record (retrieved from a fire) of Rose Kelly's time of confinement on the day I was born. It showed the time as being 1.45pm. So Mary was heading into her interview 74 years to the day, and hour, that Rose was giving birth to me. For the first time ever, I had linked into the pain of the mother or father who, for whatever reason, had had to walk away from their child; perhaps giving up any right to ever come back into their child's life again. The mixture of emotions I was experiencing that day was horrendous. Not even when I was journeying into my own history back in '96 did I feel like this. I suppose the main difference was that, for a change, it was Rose Kelly and those women like her (and even their partners, if they had one) that were taking centre stage in my thoughts. For once, it wasn't all about me.

Mary was approved as a prospective adoptive parent by the board that day; she was over the moon. We had been waiting in a local restaurant, not knowing how she would be when she joined us, but everyone was so excited and I just wondered to myself how Mammy and Daddy would have felt had they still been alive. I have absolutely no doubt that both would have been rejoicing with us if they had been there. But, then again, I know that they were, in spirit.

Christmas came and Christmas went, and so did the New Year, but still no word of any child arriving. Then spring came. As we headed into summer time, it was not just Mary but all of us eagerly awaiting news of any baby coming our way. Finally, as June moved towards its end days, Mary came home from school. Clare, our daughter-in-law, was with her. I was just putting out the dinner and I asked Mary if she had some sort of homing device linked up to the house because she always seemed to know the exact time dinner would be ready. I was laughing about that when Clare said we should sit down.

I said to her, 'why, are you pregnant or what?'

She said, 'you better sit down; Mary has something to tell you'.

We both sat down and Mary told us that she had just received a call from the adoption team telling her that she had been approved to be the mother of a baby boy who had been with his foster parent for a year or so. He was around one year and five months old: this was very much the age that I would have been when I first came to Derry and into the lives of the wider McCallion and McCourt families.

The parallels between us were increasing, day by day, and the connection was growing stronger. On an earlier occasion, I had jokingly said I hoped this child, whoever he or she may be, better not think, for one moment, that they would steal my thunder. Now, I was beginning to believe that he would; and that was OK with me. To say that the dinner was ruined that night would be an understatement; we couldn't speak, never mind eat. Well, I couldn't, anyway, because the mixed emotions welled up within me again. This time it was all about how Mammy and Daddy must have felt when I first came to them. How did I settle into the new surroundings and how would the new baby take to us? What did the future hold for Mary and the baby as they set out together in life? These were some of the questions running through my mind at that time, and believe me, there were many more on top of them.

One thing I have learned in life is this: too much analysis leads to paralysis. So, as we eagerly awaited the arrival of our fourteenth grandchild (with the thirteen before him having already claimed their very own space within our hearts), I vowed I would try not to dwell too long on what lay ahead for them both. I would just enjoy the gift of this moment, and all that it held for us all in the years that lay ahead.

Up To The Present

In 2017, when I wrote the previous chapter, I honestly thought my book was finally done (not for the first time, I hear you cry). Well, for one reason or another, I never got around to having it published. So... I have taken up my pen one last time. As I write, it is late November, 2022. I am fast approaching my 80th birthday. Little did I think, when I began the journey into my birth origins 26 years ago, that I would still be dealing with the fallout today (though not in a bad way, I must add).

Just like our parents before us, Sally and I have grown older; we are now watching our own children undergo the same experiences with their children that we had with them. They are now the ones watching the younger generation make their way in the real world, venturing along the highway of life with all of its twists and turns and its highs and lows. These last few years have taken us all down the road lesser travelled - especially with the onset of the Covid pandemic. Earlier in the book, I mentioned the tragic story uncovered by Dan McClernon and myself, in the course of our family research, of the Lyons family, who lost six children to the Spanish flu pandemic that killed at least 30 million people at the end of the First World War. Little did I think, back then, that the year 2020 would see another pandemic hit the world once more, or that it would also, tragically, cost millions of people their lives. Or, indeed, that we would still be dealing with the fallout from it as 2022 draws to a close.

Like every other family, we have had our experiences of having to isolate from others during these last few years. Sally was one of those people considered as being at high risk should they contract coronavirus. I was also rated as vulnerable because of my COPD. This meant we had to stick to the strict shielding guidelines issued by the government in those early, anxiety-laden days.

We got through the early months without any health problems, but then, two days before Christmas of 2020, Sally had a very bad fall which caused her to be hospitalised in the early hours of Christmas Eve. What followed was an experience I wouldn't wish on any family. For the first ten days or so, none of us was allowed into the hospital to visit Sally; not even me. We got updates about her condition by phone. Then one of us was allowed to visit Sally for a short period of time, in the hope that we could get her to eat something. That came to an end as Sally showed some signs of improvement, but it was to be another week or so before she was allowed home. To this day, Sally doesn't recall anything about her time in hospital.

Our family was totally supportive of us throughout this time, but none more so than Mary. She and the 'wee man' (that is how I will refer to him, for the sake of confidentiality) had moved in with us. Without them, I just don't know how we would have managed. Schools were closed, non-essential businesses were shut down indefinitely and all sporting activities were suspended; the world seemed to be grinding to a halt.

We had to avail of home delivery services for essential food requirements and anything else we needed to see us through those life-changing times. Don't get me wrong; we had so much to be thankful for. We had each other, the wains were in constant contact with us, and Sally and I were in contact with our siblings and their families throughout those months of the lockdown. I always thought Catherine and her family must have found this an awful time to go through, because, although they could speak to us on the phone or video call us, they couldn't actually come to our front window and look in at us like the others could.

During this time, the wee man was becoming more central to everything that was going on with us, particularly since our other grandchildren were growing older and starting to make their way through third-level education. Between them, they have more degrees than some of us have had hot dinners. As grandparents, it is fair to say that we are very proud of all that they have achieved in life and we know they will continue to fulfil their dreams in the years that lie ahead.

What can I say about the wee man who came into our lives in such a very special way? I find that the parallel between his journey and mine has created a very special bond between us, to such an extent that, at times, I have to remind myself this is his journey; not mine being repeated. I hope that makes sense to anyone who may be reading this piece of musing on my part.

We have watched him growing into the gift that keeps on giving, and the love that calls us into action, as he has gone through the different stages of development; from the baby who came into our midst in the summer of 2017 to the wee boy of today who has stolen a large chunk of our hearts.

Like all his cousins, he has inherited his granda's sense of humour, and therefore loves teasing his nanny any chance he gets. We have had the joy of witnessing all the different stages of play that children his age go through. He used to come in and say, 'Granda and Nanny, we are playing Ninja Warriors today'. We also went through the dinosaur stage and he never failed to amaze us with his knowledge of all the different kinds that had ever roamed the earth. Indeed, any form of play that took his fancy over the passing years, we have been there to enjoy with him.

We have had the honour of taking him to and collecting him from crèche, then nursery school and now primary school. We watched his baby teeth grow and now we are watching them start to fall out. We have seen his excitement when the fairies left him a gold coin in exchange for his baby tooth that he had put under his pillow the night before.

Most amazing of all, we have witnessed him transform from the timid baby he was when he came to us into the assured wee boy he has grown into over the last few years (and who, in a given situation, can once again become the baby of yore). We have been very much a part of all his birthday and Christmas celebrations. Just like the rest of our grandchildren, he takes total delight in the fact that, when I open my present from Santa, it is always a bag of coal because I wasn't a good boy.

It is fair to say that, because we are both older and are now retired, the wee man has seen more of us than our own children (or any of our other grandchildren) ever have, and at times that saddens me. But I can come to terms with that thinking by reminding myself that the role of the grandparent is so different from that of the parent, who has to ensure there is food on the table to feed the hungry, money in the pot to help clothe the growing offspring and a balanced outlook on life to help guide their children onwards and upwards, working towards their own destiny, so they can enhance their individual career prospects.

I often wondered how I would know when (or indeed if) the wee man would ever accept us as his grandparents. Well, for me it was the day that he called out to me from the toilet, 'Granda, you can clean my bum'.

In 2020, we had a double celebration, one day after the other, for Mary's 40th and Catherine's 50th birthdays. What made it even more special was that just days beforehand, the wee man's adoption had finally been approved by the courts. He was baptised on Mary's birthday. It literally was the icing on the cake for all of us, but none more so than for Mary herself.

There has been sadness, too. A great sense of loss was felt by our entire family (none of us more so than Sally) when Gena, the wife of Sally's late brother Michael, passed away on June 8, 2021.

Also... I need to address something I never mentioned at any stage in my musings over the past 26 years. That isn't to say it has never been on my mind, because, believe me, I have gone on many a guilt trip over the years (survivor's guilt syndrome, they call it) as to why I was one of the lucky ones who escaped. By that I mean the ongoing horrendous revelations about the mother and baby homes and the institutional orphanages set up by the churches and the state and the physical, mental and sexual abuse of the children and young adults who were entrusted into their so-called care. It angers me when I think of the demeaning treatment and ostracism of the so-called 'fallen women' (among whom may very well have been my own birth mother, Rose) who were unfortunate enough to find themselves pregnant and imprisoned within those walls by those who claimed to be doing God's work. Why did so many members of the clergy and other religious orders (and laypeople, for that matter) stay silent? Particularly those who must have known about the satanic attacks on the helpless victims and, no doubt, about the identities of those who were perpetrating these ungodly actions.

It also angers me to think about the apathy of successive governments and various political parties (on both sides of the border) down through the years. This was surely a betrayal - on all levels of humanity - of all that is decent and morally correct. I also question, within my mind, how any God-fearing man or woman within the clerical or religious orders, entrusted with the saving of souls, can abuse the victims all over again by denying them the truth, the whole truth, and nothing but the truth. There are records in existence that must be opened up so that the captives can at last (and in their lifetimes) be set free. Thanks be to God, the people of the religious orders who were central to my search were certainly not of that ilk. Indeed, I count many of them as close personal friends.

Another scandal dating back to times long gone is of the children (girls and boys) who found themselves being transported - yes, transported - to faraway places all over the world; supposedly to improve their opportunities in life. One only has to read of the traumatic abuse and tragic experiences suffered by those who were part of this enforced migration for us to realise the damage caused to these poor victims/ survivors.

Then came the horrendous and earth-shattering discovery of the fate of children who had died at the Bon Secours mother and baby home in Tuam, Galway; their wee bodies dumped into a tank within the grounds of the convent. It is hard to fathom the mindset (much less the soul) of a person who could carry out acts of such indescribable cruelty.

I believe the actions (or rather, inaction) of the present government, as well as those members of the ongoing redress scheme, have not been nearly good enough. How can decisions to lock certain files away for years - files relating to the records of these institutions - be justifiable on any level? It is, indeed, time for the truth to be told.

Back to the present. If the last few years have taught us anything, it must be (in my opinion, anyway) that we should live for today, and all that it holds, and keep all that is precious to us close. And what is more precious than the love and support of family and friends? It is the glue that keeps us together in the midst of what, at times, would seem to be a mad, mad world.

The Final Reflection

More than twenty years ago, I wrote that maybe someone else might finish this book. I said that because I believed, back then, that my input was complete. But, with the passing of time, I came to realise that it certainly wasn't over. I believed that, when the child took his place on the platform to speak, there wouldn't be anything left to be said - especially by the man. How wrong was I? The man of that time, I now know, hid behind the shadow of the child.

He let him take centre stage, but the child could only reflect on his experiences of their early years. So I, the man, now know that it is time for me to reflect; not just on the initial journey but on all that has unfolded since then. So here goes...

During the intense, hectic rush of my search to find Rose, I kept a daily diary. It recorded the frantic, unfolding revelations of my hidden past and my manic emotional reactions to what I was seeing as denial and rejection from different sources. I did this because I knew that, if I tried to deal with it all at once, I would have had a breakdown (though, in some odd way, I did anyway). It was as if I was putting all the revelations into pigeonholes so that I could go back later and remove them, one by one, and slowly try to make sense of all that had taken place in such a short space of time.

Little did I think, twenty-odd years on, that I would still be dealing with the contents of those daily entries in my diary. I am still dealing with the fallout from those pigeonholes because they can still intrude into my life; with subtlety, and often quite unexpectedly. It could even be a word spoken, a thought broken or, indeed, a sudden flash of days and people long gone, and the turmoil from that time would make its way back to the surface of my thinking. I have struggled, and pondered deeply, as to how I could get myself sufficiently focused and detached so that I could find the best starting point for this reflection. I have decided to use one of the many musings that I wrote along the way. It goes like this:

A Bird It Can Sing
With A Broken Wing

Life has taken me where I didn't want to be,
Shown me things that I didn't want to see,
There's no easy road, no way to ease the load,
Once the roller coaster's free.

Chorus
But a bird it can sing with a broken wing,
But not with a broken heart,
Yes, a bird it can sing with a broken wing,
But not with a broken heart.

Because of all my fears, and all my hidden tears,
I've built me a wall, thick and tall,
No one may enter there, to see me standing bare,
No mask to hide my pain, I'm on my own.

Chorus
But a bird it can sing etc.

It's time to move along, to go and sing my song,
Time to claim all that's me,
So, Lord, please heal this heart, then you can make a start,
To set this little bird free.

Then this bird he will sing, there'll be no broken wing,
For the Lord can heal all of me,
Yes, this bird he will sing, there'll be no broken wing,
And the Lord, He will set me free.

Chorus

At the start of this journey (and many times during it), I was guilt-ridden with the sense of betrayal. Not of me, the child, being betrayed, but betrayal by me of those who had shown me what true love really was: Mammy and Daddy. Truth be told, I didn't want to damage my relationship with them in any way.

I also had mixed emotions regarding Rose. I wanted to tell her that the decision she made to give me up for adoption had turned out to be the right one but I felt guilty that I couldn't relate to her as my mother. That right belonged to Mammy, and Mammy only.

As the walls of secrecy began to tumble down, there were times I wanted to get away from the whole situation (as far and as quickly as I could) but the roller coaster had been set in motion. On several occasions, when things were becoming too much for me to deal with and I had decided to pack it all in, something deep within me would well up again and drive me onwards and upwards... even as it showed me the things I didn't want to see.

What were those things, one may well ask? Well, there were several that come to mind, even now. For example, I didn't want to find that she had had other children; not because I would be jealous of their mother-child relationship but because I didn't want the possible complications that might result from that information. They might be expecting me to form some kind of sibling connection but I already had that with Nuala, Kevin and Marian. So it would only complicate things between the four of us; maybe even result in blurring the lines between us as siblings and I certainly didn't want that.

But a bird it can sing. Well, not always; there were many times in the early days, and on many occasions over the following years, that I found it hard to sing. Anyone who knows me, especially those who live with me, would tell you that I drive them mad, at times, with my incessant singing around the house - sometimes without me even realising I am singing. But the bird (me) had not just a broken wing back then, but also an aching heart to go with it because of some of the stuff that was being revealed.

The bottom line was that no one seemed to know I existed and that Rose had four other children. The worse thing of all was that she didn't seem to have told anyone of my existence. I could have been in Australia, for all she knew; sure I was Mr Nobody.

I was the beautiful Easter egg that everyone wished for but found that when the wrapping had been removed from it, it was broken into many, many pieces. That was how I felt... and it was an awful feeling to have.

But I knew that I had reached a point in my journey where I had to move on. I had to claim back all of me, because if I didn't I would never be free.

I was blessed to have my own guardian angel walking by my side, both night and day. Her name (if you haven't already guessed it) is Sally. Sally was the one who bore the brunt of most of my mood swings. She was the one who knew when I needed space - even when I was in a crowd. She was the one who, only once, said she was sorry I had gone on this journey, not because of the stress she was obviously feeling but because of what it was doing to me.

I was also lucky to have several good friends to whom I could go when I thought that Sally needed some space.

It was with the help of Sally, and the close friends who were Godsends in my time of need, that I finally began to feel that God was setting me free.

I have learned that, though my heart may break with pain, it will expand with love; and love can move mountains that may seem to be immovable. I say this because the doors that were once closed have now all been opened wide, and friendships that I didn't even expect to make are now encased in gold, metaphorically speaking.

Again, something that still amazes me is that, after the early days of my search and the many surprises that I had along the way, things are still being uncovered that add to what I know of Rose; at the most unexpected times, and in the most mysterious ways. I say this because on the day of my 74th birthday, I became totally aware - for the first time ever - of the pain that my Wild Irish Rose must have suffered when she had to (for whatever reason) walk away from me and leave me to the waves of the world. Because I knew she couldn't do any better at that time.

The pain that I felt then was a pain that was festering for a long time, but it was a pain that I couldn't have dealt with earlier in my life - and certainly not during my journey. I knew, once again, that it was in God's time, and that it was His way of caring for me and mine.

Yes, this life has taken me to where I didn't want to be and has shown me things that I didn't want to see. But today, looking back, I can honestly say I wouldn't change a thing. For I have come to realise that it was because of those times, and other life experiences, that I am the man I am today.

EPILOGUE

At the start of 2022, we welcomed the first of our next generation into our family: a beautiful, bouncing baby girl called Aya. She is the daughter of our granddaughter Sarah and her partner Micheál. In a matter of months, she wove her way into the heartstrings of everyone blessed to have met her - and continues to do so. She has the most disarming smile and beautiful eyes, both of which light up any room she decides to grace with her presence.

To add to this joy, my youngest sister Marian had planned to come back to Derry in July to celebrate her 70th birthday along with her husband Michael, their three boys and their partners and the grandchildren.

My sister Nuala and her husband Michael also planned to get here for the celebrations. It had been a while since we had all been together, which in itself added to the occasion.

Then life threw one of its curve balls into the mix that drastically changed everything: Marian and Michael's youngest son, Simon, passed away in the middle of June after a very short illness.

None of us can begin to imagine how devastating the loss of Simon from their everyday lives is for Marian, Michael, Mark and Kevin, but especially for Simon's young son Ethan. Nor can we begin to understand the agonising decision they had to make when, as his next of kin, they had to decide if Simon's organs should be made available for transplant or not.

The law in England around organ transplants had changed so that everyone is considered a willing donor unless their next of kin decide otherwise. So his Mammy, Daddy and brother Mark were now asked to make the final decision regarding Simon's organs.

Needless to say, they considered what Simon would want them to do, and they now know that four people have had life-changing transplants because of their generosity of mind and heart, and despite their own tremendous pain at Simon's going from their midst. Now, all we can do is be there for them - even though we are so far apart - whenever the need arises.

Marian and Michael did come to Derry, and I hope and pray that they all found some solace and comfort during their time back here.

Towards the tail end of 2022, we were looking forward to the arrival of our second great-grandchild, who was due at the end of January 2023. Well, they say that if you want to give God a laugh, tell him your plans for the next few days. In our case, it was for the next several weeks, because our great-grandchild decided he wasn't for waiting until 2023, and instead made his grand entrance into all our lives on December 4th. Obviously, it was a time of great concern - especially for his mammy and daddy (my granddaughter Caoimhe and her partner Sean) - as he was born by Caesarian and weighed just 3lbs 12oz.

But Jamie Mark McGrath is a mighty wee warrior. He was released from the hospital on December 21st and we finally got to see him and hold him in our arms on Christmas Day when Caoimhe and Sean brought him to our house. It was an amazing feeling and it certainly added to the specialness of the Christmas season.

And so the story of our lives goes on and on, through the arrival of the younger generation into our midst.

December 2022 was also momentous in another way; I celebrated my 80th birthday. We had hired out the function room of a local hotel so that we could gather with our family and some friends, but Sally wasn't keeping the best, as they say, so we decided just to stay at home and keep it to close family. I didn't want her to feel pressured in any way, so it was my decision to cancel the hotel.

Catherine and Pat came up from their home in Macroom. Our grandchildren, Molly, Kate and Finn, were unable to come because of work, university and school commitments, and Emmet's children, Marie and Kevin, were also unable to come because of their work commitments in England.

But I had a very special birthday. The wee man was the first to land, insisting he wanted to sing happy birthday to me before the others arrived. I now have a very special video of him doing so, along with a memory no one can ever erase from my mind of him running to me and giving me a very, very special hug.

The others started arriving after five o'clock and they didn't leave until after 11. I was totally shattered, and realised that I really couldn't have been up to the hotel situation.

The following day I still felt like a wet rag - this from a man who didn't even have an alcoholic drink during my birthday celebrations!

As I look back over those 80 years, one thought I have is that I hope my wild Irish Rose is proud of what I have done with the only gift she could give me when she found herself pregnant with me back in 1942... the gift of life.

Today, as I reflect on what might have been if Mammy and Daddy hadn't said yes to God's plan for them to be the parents of the four of us, coming from different places and knitting us into a family, I thank God from the bottom of my heart for their selflessness.

Johnny McCallion
February 2023

ACKNOWLEDGEMENTS

Firstly, I want to acknowledge three people who each played a very big part in my search for and eventual discovery of Rose. The first is the lady who I went to on the day I realised I had to do something to help me get over the stressful situation that I was in: Sr Bernadine. The second was Fr Frank O'Hagan, who helped me put the pieces of the jigsaw together and the third was Eva White, the lady in the registry office in Belfast, who was so kind and helpful when I decided to search for my birth records and those of Rose.

Every so often, we come across kindred spirits, and that certainly was the case when I met Fiona Tope and, later, her husband Martin. They were the present-day replica of my parents as they, too, had adopted their children. We met through our involvement with the Holy Family parish (by the way, Fiona was my unpaid secretary in the early days and typed up my notes for me).

My friends Kevin and Geraldine Glackin gave me support and whatever else I needed during many troubled and trying times. They weren't slow to give me a kick up the backside whenever the 'poor me' syndrome appeared.

Another port of call was the home of Martin and Eileen McLaughlin, my friends from the Derry Search group. There was always a welcome mat, for me or anyone who knocked at their door, both night and day. Martin was also my boss, and I certainly am grateful for the support he gave to me to allow me to carry out my search for Rose and her origins.

I have spoken at length about my late, great friend Johnnie White, but behind every great man is a great woman; in this case, his wife Doreen. She never once gave me the impression that I was an intruder or a nuisance whenever I called unexpectedly and dragged Johnnie off to somewhere quiet, to discuss whatever my latest crisis was in my search for Rose.

Marie Doherty and the rest of the Doherty clan of Carrickreagh Gardens was one family I could always call with, no matter what may have been troubling me. Why? The answer to that one is very simple: because my troubles always seemed to be a lot lighter by the time I was leaving them. I will always be indebted to Marie and them for that.

I thank Sr Anna Doherty, from the bottom of my heart, for the encouragement she gave me to undertake several courses in faith formation, some of them at the same time, despite my initial reluctance to do so back then. She helped deepen my faith in God, but also - maybe more importantly - my faith in myself.

I want to thank two people who helped me get this book published: my editor, Mary-Anne McNulty, pulled my story together in a beautiful way, while graphic designer Patrick Leonard brought great expertise and professionalism to the finished product.

I'd also like to express my gratitude to two people, each of whom helped me get things in order at different stages in the process. To Kathleen Kerrigan and Pádraig McConway; thank you.

I am very fortunate to have come into contact with Dan McClernon, who shared with me the treasure trove of his grandmother's letters and photos. It is thanks to him that I have photos of Rose and her family spanning the years from her childhood into adulthood. Dan and I have forged a deep friendship as a result.

Obviously, the most important support I received was from my own family. Edward, Stephen, Emmet, Catherine and Mary, despite the effect it must have had on them, were always behind me. Maybe one day they may decide to tell how my journey impacted on their lives - but that is entirely up to them.

Now we come to the big one. The rock on which I am built, the foundation on which I stand firm, the lady who held me in her arms when the going got tough. Even those times when she wanted me to give up the search, not because of what it was doing to her (oh no) but because of what it was doing to me, she never faltered in her support. Sally, I thought I knew what love was all about, but during these 57 years of married life you have never failed to amaze me with your capacity to love beyond all human understanding. I am forever thankful to the God who brought us together, and for the undying love that you have given to me from the day you said 'yes', that you would be my wife.

Finally, to anyone in the wider Kelly clan who may have found the suddenness of my intrusion into your space in any way hard to deal with, I apologise. It was never my intention to do harm or upset anyone. All I ever wanted to do was to thank Rose, when she couldn't give me anything else, for giving me the gift of life, and to tell her that her decision to give me up for adoption has been the right one for me.

I pray that my Wild Irish Rose now has a peace only God could give her.

Printed in Great Britain
by Amazon

21778338R00157